Exploring English
GRAMMAR

E

Continental

Credits

Illustrations: Laurie Conley, Eric Hammond, Margaret Lindmark, David Stirba, Meryl Treatner, Carolyn Williams

ISBN 978-1-5240-0267-1

Copyright © 2017 The Continental Press, Inc.

No part of this publication may be reproduced in any form or by any means, electronic, mechanical, photocopying, recording, or otherwise, without the prior written permission of the publisher. All rights reserved. Printed in the United States of America.

Table of Contents

Introduction to *Exploring English Grammar* 5

UNIT 1 Sentences
Lesson 1	**Sentences and Fragments**	6
Lesson 2	**Subject**	8
Lesson 3	**Predicate**	10
Lesson 4	**Types of Sentences**	12
Lesson 5	**Run-On Sentences**	14
Lesson 6	**Conjunctions and Interjections**	16
Lesson 7	**Compound Subjects and Predicates**	18
Lesson 8	**Compound Sentences**	20

UNIT 2 Nouns
Lesson 1	**Nouns**	22
Lesson 2	**Possessive Nouns**	24
Lesson 3	**Plural Forms**	26
Lesson 4	**Irregular Plural Forms**	28
Lesson 5	**Abstract Nouns**	30

UNIT 3 Verbs
Lesson 1	**Action Verbs**	32
Lesson 2	**Direct Objects**	34
Lesson 3	**Linking and Helping Verbs**	36
Lesson 4	**Simple Future and Present Tense**	38
Lesson 5	**Simple Past Tense**	40
Lesson 6	**Simple Past Tense: Irregular Forms**	42
Lesson 7	**Progressive Tense**	44
Lesson 8	**Perfect Tense**	46
Lesson 9	**Perfect Tense with Irregular Past Participles**	48

UNIT 4 Pronouns
Lesson 1	**Subject and Object Pronouns**	50
Lesson 2	**Possessive Pronouns**	52
Lesson 3	**Relative Pronouns**	54
Lesson 4	***Self*-Pronouns**	56

UNIT 5 Adjectives and Adverbs

Lesson 1	Adjectives and Articles	58
Lesson 2	Comparing with Adjectives	60
Lesson 3	More Comparing with Adjectives	62
Lesson 4	Order of Adjectives	64
Lesson 5	Adverbs	66
Lesson 6	Comparing with Adverbs	68

UNIT 6 Phrases, Clauses, and Complex Sentences

Lesson 1	Prepositional Phrases	70
Lesson 2	Independent and Dependent Clauses	72
Lesson 3	Complex Sentences	74
Lesson 4	Misplaced Modifiers	76

UNIT 7 Capital Letters

Lesson 1	Beginning a Sentence or a Direct Quotation	78
Lesson 2	Proper Nouns and Titles of Respect	80
Lesson 3	Titles of Works	82

UNIT 8 Punctuation and Style

Lesson 1	End Punctuation and Other Uses of a Period	84
Lesson 2	Comma	86
Lesson 3	Apostrophe	88
Lesson 4	Writing Direct Quotations	90
Lesson 5	Colon, Semicolon, and Dash	92
Lesson 6	Writing Titles of Works	94

UNIT 9 Choosing the Right Word

Lesson 1	Homophones	96
Lesson 2	More Homophones	98
Lesson 3	Avoiding Double Negatives	100
Lesson 4	Misused Words	102
Lesson 5	More Misused Words	104

UNIT 10 Writing Letters

Lesson 1	Writing a Thank-You Note	106
Lesson 2	Writing a Business Letter	108
Lesson 3	Addressing an Envelope	110
Lesson 4	Writing an Email	112

Grammar Handbook 114

Introduction to
Exploring English Grammar

You use language every day to speak, listen, read, and write. Using language effectively helps you to communicate your thoughts and ideas to those around you. To understand and use the English language, you must understand and use the rules of grammar. Knowing parts of speech, punctuation, sentence structure, and capitalization rules helps you to master the English language. *Exploring English Grammar* reviews important language rules to help you grow into a skillful communicator.

Exploring English Grammar includes skills in the following areas:

- Sentence structure
- Nouns
- Verbs
- Verb tenses
- Pronouns
- Adjectives
- Adverbs
- Types of sentences
- Capitalization
- Punctuation
- Word usage
- Letter writing

Lesson 1

UNIT 1: Sentences
Sentences and Fragments

Remember A **sentence** is a group of words that tells a complete thought. If the words do not tell a complete thought, they are a **fragment.**

Sentence   Abraham Lincoln was born in Kentucky.
Fragment   Abraham Lincoln.
Sentence   His family moved to Indiana.
Fragment   Moved to Indiana.

Think About What is the difference between a sentence and a fragment?

_____

_____

Read and Apply Read the groups of words. Write **S** above the first word of each sentence. Write **F** above each fragment.

The Underground Railroad. No trains ran on it. Its stations were daytime hiding places. Led slaves. At night. One famous conductor. She had once been a slave herself. The Ohio River separated the slave states from the free states. The river to freedom. Men, women, and children. Thousands of slaves escaped between 1830 and 1860.

© The Continental Press, Inc.   DUPLICATING THIS MATERIAL IS ILLEGAL.

Write About Write a paragraph about a place you have been that you did not like very much. Be sure to use sentences that express complete thoughts.

___

Review Read each fragment. Correct the fragment by writing it as a complete sentence.

1. Hiding in the woods.

2. Many kind people.

3. Not safe.

4. Barns, fields, and houses.

Lesson 2: Subject

Remember A sentence has two parts. The **subject** tells who or what the sentence is about. The **simple subject** is the noun or pronoun in the subject. The **complete subject** is that main word and all of the words that tell about it.

complete subject ↓
The people of this city voted for a new mayor.
simple subject ↑

Think About What is the difference between the simple subject and the complete subject?

_____

_____

Read and Apply Read the sentences. Underline the complete subject in each one. Circle the simple subject.

Small fires are nature's way of helping the forest. Weak old trees are cleared away by these fires. New young plants have room to grow. Forest fires can get too big. Many hardworking, brave people must fight to get them under control.

Most plants can survive forest fires. The roots of grass are underground, away from the fire. Many pine trees grow special cones full of resin. This material protects the seeds inside the cones from fire. Most animals will flee from forest fires.

Write About Write a paragraph about what you think it would be like to fight a forest fire. Underline the complete subject in each of your sentences.

_____
_____
_____
_____
_____
_____
_____
_____
_____

Review Read each sentence. The complete subject is underlined once. The simple subject is underlined twice. Check the box for **YES** if the sentence is marked correctly. Check the box for **NO** if it is not marked correctly.

1. The dry climate of Southern California leads to many wildfires. YES ☐ NO ☐

2. Almost one million people had to leave their homes during the 2007 wildfires. YES ☐ NO ☐

3. Strong winds cause the fires to spread. YES ☐ NO ☐

4. Special aircraft help firefighters. YES ☐ NO ☐

5. Many wildfires in the United States are caused by people. YES ☐ NO ☐

© The Continental Press, Inc. DUPLICATING THIS MATERIAL IS ILLEGAL.

Lesson 3: Predicate

Remember The second part of a sentence is the predicate. The **predicate** tells what the subject does or is. The **simple predicate** is the verb or verb phrase in the predicate. The **complete predicate** is that main word or phrase and all of the words that tell about it.

complete predicate ↓
A Swiss person may speak French, German, Italian, or Romansh.
simple predicate ↑

Think About In the example above, is the simple predicate a verb or a verb phrase? How do you know?

_____

_____

Read and Apply Read the sentences. Underline the complete predicate in each one. Circle the simple predicate.

Wang Yani's paintings show birds, monkeys, and flowers. This woman from China began painting before the age of 3. Her father recognized her talent quickly. He was eager to encourage her work. One of Wang Yani's paintings appeared on a postage stamp in China when she was 4. Museums and galleries displayed her artwork by the time she was 13.

Wang Yani paints with a traditional Chinese style and technique. Her brush seems to dance across the paper. She makes bold strokes of ink on the paper. Beautiful scenes and animals almost leap from the pictures.

© The Continental Press, Inc. **DUPLICATING THIS MATERIAL IS ILLEGAL.**

Write About Write a paragraph about an art form that you enjoy looking at or doing. Underline the complete predicate in each of your sentences.

_____
_____
_____
_____
_____
_____
_____
_____
_____

Review Read each sentence. The complete predicate is underlined once. The simple predicate is underlined twice. Check the box for **YES** if the sentence is marked correctly. Check the box for **NO** if it is not marked correctly.

1. The Smithsonian Institution <u>displayed Wang Yani's work</u>.   YES ☐   NO ☐

2. Crowds of people <u>gathered to watch her paint</u>.   YES ☐   NO ☐

3. Wang Yani's paintings <u>often show playful monkeys</u>.   YES ☐   NO ☐

4. Six books <u>have been written about Wang Yani</u>.   YES ☐   NO ☐

5. People <u>still enjoy looking at Wang Yani's paintings</u>.   YES ☐   NO ☐

Lesson 4: Types of Sentences

Remember There are four kinds of sentences. A **declarative** sentence states or tells something and ends with a **period (.)**. An **interrogative** sentence asks a question and ends with a **question mark (?)**. An **exclamatory** sentence shows surprise or strong feeling and ends with an **exclamation point (!)**. An **imperative** sentence asks or commands someone to do something. It usually ends with a period, but it can end with an exclamation point.

Declarative   New York is our country's largest city.
Interrogative   What was it like 400 years ago?
Exclamatory   How quiet it must have been!
Imperative   Try to imagine who might have lived there.

Think About What type of imperative sentence will end in an exclamation point? Give an example.

_____

_____

Read and Apply Read the sentences. Above each one, write an abbreviation to tell what kind it is. Use decl. for declarative, inter. for interrogative, excl. for exclamatory, and imp. for imperative.

Do you know what a therapy dog is? It is a dog that visits people in hospitals and nursing homes. How bored some of those patients are! Some may be sad or depressed. How happy it makes them to see a dog! How is a therapy dog different from ordinary dogs? It has to be specially trained. It cannot jump up on people. Imagine what a special dog it must be! Studies show that therapy dogs help patients feel better physically. Think about how happy you feel when petting a dog.

Write About Write four sentences you might say to a dog. Write one of each kind of sentence.

_____
_____
_____
_____
_____
_____
_____

Review Listen to each sentence. Circle the type of sentence it is. Circle **DECL** for declarative, **INTER** for interrogative, **EXCL** for exclamatory, and **IMP** for imperative.

1. DECL   INTER   EXCL   IMP
2. DECL   INTER   EXCL   IMP
3. DECL   INTER   EXCL   IMP
4. DECL   INTER   EXCL   IMP
5. DECL   INTER   EXCL   IMP
6. DECL   INTER   EXCL   IMP

Lesson 5: Run-On Sentences

Remember A sentence tells just one complete thought. If two or more thoughts are run together, the group of words is not a sentence. It is a **run-on**.

Run-On Amy Beach was an American composer she wrote many beautiful pieces of music.

Sentences Amy Beach was an American composer. She wrote many beautiful pieces of music.

Think About How are run-ons separated to make sentences?

_____

_____

Read and Apply Read the sentences. Underline the run-ons.

   Duke Ellington was one of the greatest American composers of all time. He learned to play piano at a young age and wrote his first song when he was 15. After high school, Duke decided to become a musician he formed a band and played in New York City. In the 1940s, his jazz music was very popular. His songs covered a wide range of sounds and rhythms there was often a story behind the music, too.

   In his lifetime, Duke composed over 3,000 songs and was known around the world. He won 13 Grammy Awards he also received both the President's Gold Medal and the Presidential Medal of Freedom. Duke's songs remain an important part of American culture many people still sing and listen to them today.

Write About Look at the run-ons you found in Read and Apply. Write each one correctly. Use end punctuation and a capital letter to separate the sentences.

_____
_____
_____
_____
_____
_____
_____
_____
_____

Review Read these run-ons. Write each one correctly.

1. Why did people call him Duke it was because he was gentlemanly.
   _____
   _____

2. Listen to the trumpet, piano, and saxophone how great they sound!
   _____
   _____

3. One of Duke's famous songs is "Mood Indigo" do you know it?
   _____
   _____

Lesson 6: Conjunctions and Interjections

Remember A **conjunction** is a word that connects words or groups of words in a sentence.

Martin <u>and</u> Sylvia visited Alaska. They had never seen a glacier <u>or</u> a fur seal <u>before</u>. They enjoyed their trip, <u>but</u> they were glad to get <u>home</u>.

Correlative conjunctions are used in pairs. They connect two equal grammatical parts in a sentence.

We could take <u>either</u> the train <u>or</u> the bus.

The movie was <u>neither</u> interesting <u>nor</u> funny.

Interjections are words that show strong or sudden feeling. Some interjections are sounds.

<u>Hey</u>! Watch where you are going!

<u>Mmmm</u>, this tastes delicious.

Think About What is the difference between conjunctions and correlative conjunctions?

_____

_____

Read and Apply Read the sentences. Circle the conjunctions. Underline the interjection.

A laser beam is a tiny and powerful ray of light. It is very concentrated, but it produces great heat. Doctors and surgeons use lasers. The light burns damaged tissue away but doesn't harm healthy tissue at all. The Army and the Navy use lasers, too. A beam can be aimed at an enemy airplane or ship to find its speed and distance. Welders and carpenters use lasers to cut materials. You might use a laser in either a printer or a scanner.

Amazing! Lasers are even used for entertainment. Laser light shows and laser tag are exciting and fun!

Write About Write a paragraph about an invention or discovery that has made your life different from your grandparents' lives. Then circle each conjunction in your sentences. Use at least one interjection.

_____
_____
_____
_____
_____
_____
_____
_____

Review Write a conjunction or an interjection in each blank to complete the sentences.

1. Dentists use lasers to treat tooth decay _____ gum disease.

2. This laser is used _____ to cut _____ to remove.

3. _____, lasers can whiten teeth _____ harden a filling.

4. Lasers are used in many ways, _____ there is still much to learn about them.

Lesson 7

Compound Subjects and Predicates

Remember A **compound subject** or a **compound predicate** can be made by using a conjunction.

Compound Subject Seatbelts and air bags belong in every car.

Compound Predicate They prevent injuries and save lives.

Think About Read the examples again. How would the meaning of the sentences change if the conjunction *or* was used instead of *and*?

_____

_____

Read and Apply Read the sentences. Underline the compound subject or predicate in each one. Then circle the two main words in the compound part.

Most people never think about numbers but use them all the time. Store clerks and bank tellers work daily with numbers. Scientists count or figure. You and your parents use numbers, too. You shop and keep records with numbers. With them, your parents figure taxes and pay bills.

Numbers and number systems are not all alike. The Arabic system and the Roman system are the most familiar ones. But the Maya and the Chinese had interesting systems, too. The Maya were good at math and had a symbol for zero. Zeroes and fractions weren't included in the Roman system at all. The Chinese liked them both and used them often.

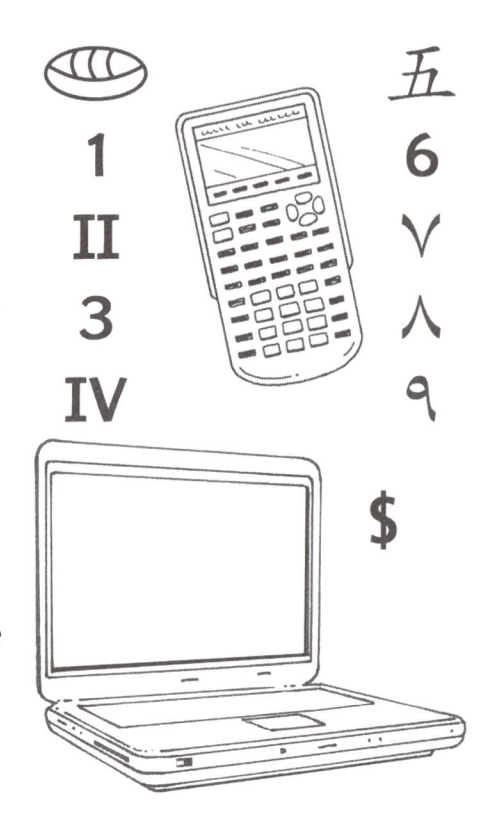

© The Continental Press, Inc. DUPLICATING THIS MATERIAL IS ILLEGAL.

Write About Write a paragraph about how you use numbers when you are not in school.

_____
_____
_____
_____
_____
_____
_____

Review Read each pair of sentences. Combine the sentences using a compound subject or a compound predicate.

1. My class learned about the Civil War. My class went on a field trip.

   _____
   _____

2. Jess went to the baseball game. Anton went to the baseball game.

   _____
   _____

3. This key opens the front door. This key locks the garage.

   _____
   _____

4. Mr. Nguyen watched the play. The other parents watched the play.

   _____
   _____

Lesson 8

Compound Sentences

Remember A simple sentence has one subject and one predicate. A **compound sentence** is two related simple sentences joined by a conjunction.

Simple Sentences Polar bears live near the North Pole. Penguins live near the South Pole.

Compound Sentence Polar bears live near the North Pole, but penguins live near the South Pole.

Think About Think about compound sentences and conjunctions. Explain when to use the conjunctions *and, or,* and *but.*

_____

_____

Read and Apply Read the sentences. Underline each compound sentence.

The Grimké sisters were famous once, but they are almost forgotten now. They were raised on a plantation in South Carolina. Their family owned slaves, but the sisters hated slavery. Sarah and Angelina Grimké decided to move to the North. There they could lead quiet lives, or they could speak out against slavery. Women were not allowed to speak in public, but they did it anyway. In 1838, Angelina Grimké spoke to the government of Massachusetts. She and her sister traveled around New England giving speeches. Their speeches drew a lot of attention. Other people joined them, and soon the lawmakers began to listen.

Write About Write a paragraph about something that you believe is wrong. Tell how you would change it.

_____
_____
_____
_____
_____
_____
_____

Review Read each pair of sentences. Combine the sentences as a compound sentence.

1. The Grimké sisters wrote about the evils of slavery. They also spoke out for women's rights.

   _____
   _____

2. They inherited slaves from their father. They freed the slaves.

   _____
   _____

3. Angelina was a strong public speaker. Both sisters were good writers.

   _____
   _____

4. Sarah wanted to be a lawyer. Her father did not allow her to go to law school.

   _____
   _____

Lesson 1

UNIT 2: Nouns

Nouns

Remember Nouns are naming words. A **common noun** names any person, place, animal, or thing. A **proper noun** names a particular person, place, animal, or thing.

Common	woman	city	horse	holiday
Proper	Megan	Atlanta	Black Beauty	Arbor Day

Think About In what way are common and proper nouns written differently?

_____

_____

Read and Apply Read the sentences. Underline each common noun. Circle each proper noun.

Cheetahs are the fastest mammals on land. These creatures can run down an antelope at 60 miles per hour. The swift hunters live in the grasslands of Africa and Asia. Long ago, kings in India hunted with these beautiful, fast cats.

Now these wild cats are in danger. The Cheetah Conservation Fund is working to save these animals. Dr. Laurie Marker founded the group. It teaches farmers in Namibia how to protect their herds without killing cheetahs. The organization also started International Cheetah Day on December 4. On this day, people look for ways to help save these amazing beings.

© The Continental Press, Inc.   DUPLICATING THIS MATERIAL IS ILLEGAL.

Write About Write a paragraph about an animal that you admire. Then circle each noun in your sentences.

_____
_____
_____
_____
_____
_____
_____
_____
_____

Review Listen to the nouns. Circle **COMMON** if it is a common noun. Circle **PROPER** if it is a proper noun.

1. COMMON   PROPER
2. COMMON   PROPER
3. COMMON   PROPER
4. COMMON   PROPER
5. COMMON   PROPER
6. COMMON   PROPER
7. COMMON   PROPER
8. COMMON   PROPER

Lesson 2: Possessive Nouns

Remember A **possessive noun** names who or what has something. It shows ownership.

<u>Ann's</u> ring   the <u>citizens'</u> votes   <u>Dr. Solomon's</u> advice

Think About How are nouns changed to make possessive forms?

_____

_____

Read and Apply Read the sentences. Underline each possessive noun.

Matthew Henson's dream was to explore the North Pole. Henson was a black farmer's son. He traveled with Robert Peary's team for 20 years and became the explorer's "first man." Peary relied on Henson's skills and knowledge. Henson spoke the Eskimos' language well. He trained the team's sled dogs and was the dogs' doctor and friend. With Henson's help, Peary reached the North Pole in 1909. The newspaper reporters' stories didn't mention Henson, though. Peary received a hero's welcome, while Matt Henson was mostly ignored.

Later, Henson wrote his memoirs of the explorations. Bradley Robinson's book, *Dark Companion,* also told of the black man's contributions. In 1944, the North Pole expedition's members received Congressional Medals. In 1988, Henson's body was moved to our country's national cemetery in Washington, DC.

Write About Write a paragraph about what places you would explore if you were an explorer.

_____
_____
_____
_____
_____
_____
_____
_____

Review Write a possessive form for each group of words.

1. the books that belong to Juan
   _____

2. the bus that belongs to the school
   _____

3. the horses that belong to the farms
   _____

4. the camera that belongs to the photographer
   _____

5. the desks that belong to the employees
   _____

6. the ball that belongs to the children
   _____

Lesson 3

Plural Forms

Remember A **singular noun** names one. A **plural noun** names more than one. Make most nouns plural by adding *s* or *es*. Sometimes you must change a letter before adding the ending.

Singular	chair	fox	city	leaf
Plural	chairs	foxes	cities	leaves

Think About Explain the four ways to make a plural noun that are shown above.

_____

_____

_____

Read and Apply Read the sentences. Find five plural nouns that are written incorrectly. Put a line through each noun and write the correct form above it.

   The enormous statues on Easter Island are one of Earth's mysteries. Early humans carved the huge faces out of solid rock. But how did the artistes move them? Each shape weighs as much as 85 tons. Archeologists think that the natives put the stone on rollers made of logs. Then they used thick ropes to pull each stone.

   The statueies are scattered over the island. Most sit with their backs to the beachs. The heads of the statues are a familiar sight. Now we know that they also have bodys buried under the ground. Some people believe the statues represent important people. At the end of their lifes, these people were buried under a statue.

Write About Write a story about how you think the islanders moved the Easter Island statues. Be creative.

_____
_____
_____
_____
_____
_____
_____
_____
_____
_____
_____

Review Write the plural form of each noun.

1. wolf _____
2. leash _____
3. hobby _____
4. dime _____
5. cavity _____

6. flea _____
7. blueberry _____
8. loaf _____
9. tax _____
10. orchard _____

© The Continental Press, Inc. **DUPLICATING THIS MATERIAL IS ILLEGAL.**

Lesson 4: Irregular Plural Forms

Remember Not all nouns follow the normal rules for plural forms. Some nouns change their spellings. Some nouns do not change at all.

Singular	man	fungus	deer	sheep
Plural	men	fungi	deer	sheep

Countable nouns can be counted using numbers. They have singular and plural forms. **Uncountable nouns** cannot be counted with numbers. They are treated as singular nouns and do not have a plural form.

uncountable ↓   countable ↓
The music sounds beautiful. These two songs are my favorites.

Think About What is a good way to learn irregular plural forms?

_____

_____

Read and Apply Read the sentences. Circle the irregular plural forms of nouns. Underline the three uncountable nouns. Use a dictionary if necessary.

   The Mojave Desert is in California. This desert gets less than 13 inches of rain each year and is the driest place in North America. Death Valley, which is 280 feet below sea level, is in the Mojave. About 2,000 species of plants and animals live in the desert. One plant is the Joshua tree, which is only found in the Mojave. Many kinds of cacti also grow in the desert.

   The Mojave Trail is a dirt road that goes through the desert. It moves between oases because water is rare. People traveled it as they moved West in the 18th and 19th centuries. Today, men and women seeking a challenge drive the trail in four-wheel drive vehicles. They must carry everything they need with them. There is no place to buy gas on the Mojave Trail.

Write About — Use the plural form of each noun in a sentence. Use a dictionary if necessary.

1. aircraft
   _____

2. ox
   _____

3. fish
   _____

Use each uncountable noun in a sentence.

4. sugar
   _____

5. news
   _____

6. money
   _____

Review — Read each sentence. Circle **YES** if the underlined noun is an uncountable noun. Circle **NO** if it is not.

1. Mom bought new furniture for the dining room.   YES   NO
2. The soup is hot!   YES   NO
3. Eat a bowl of cereal for breakfast.   YES   NO

Complete each sentence by writing the plural form of the noun in parentheses.

4. The dentist examined Caleb's _____. (tooth)

5. Roll the _____ and then move your piece. (die)

6. This river is full of _____. (trout)

© The Continental Press, Inc.   DUPLICATING THIS MATERIAL IS ILLEGAL.

Lesson 5: Abstract Nouns

Remember **Abstract nouns** are nouns that you cannot see, hear, taste, touch, or smell. Many abstract nouns are emotions, ideas, or characteristics.

love   honesty   dreams   adventure

Think About How can you decide if a noun is an abstract noun?

_____

_____

Read and Apply Read the sentences. Underline the abstract nouns.

Have you ever heard the term "Renaissance man"? It means a person who has many different talents and skills. This person also has great intelligence. One man who is considered a Renaissance man is Leonardo da Vinci. Da Vinci was not only a great painter, he was also an inventor, musician, sculptor, and mathematician. His imagination was endless. He came up with plans for a bicycle, helicopter, and airplane hundreds of years before they were actually invented.

Da Vinci did not receive much education during his childhood. But his curiosity about many things is clear. Along with his art, da Vinci filled notebooks with his ideas about science and nature. His investigations of the human body led to new knowledge of how it worked. His paintings show beauty and amazing detail. Da Vinci's *Mona Lisa* is probably the most famous painting in the world. Da Vinci never finished it though, because he was always working toward perfection.

Write About

Write a paragraph about something you would like to learn more about. What is it? Why is it interesting to you?

_____
_____
_____
_____
_____
_____
_____
_____

Review

Listen to each noun. Circle **ABSTRACT** if it is an abstract noun. Circle **NOT ABSTRACT** if it is not an abstract noun.

1. ABSTRACT   NOT ABSTRACT
2. ABSTRACT   NOT ABSTRACT
3. ABSTRACT   NOT ABSTRACT
4. ABSTRACT   NOT ABSTRACT
5. ABSTRACT   NOT ABSTRACT
6. ABSTRACT   NOT ABSTRACT

UNIT 3: Verbs
Action Verbs

Remember An **action verb** is a word that names an action. It tells what a noun does or did.

forgive   climbed   send   remembered   crushes

Think About Does a word have to name a movement to be an action verb? Explain your answer.

_____
_____
_____

Read and Apply Read the sentences. Underline the action verb in each sentence.

Cowbirds never make their own nests. Instead, they lay their eggs in other birds' nests. Then they fly away. These lazy parents never return.

The other bird hatches the cowbird's egg along with its own eggs. It raises the baby cowbird with its own babies. And the greedy cowbird chick often kicks the other babies out of the nest.

Sometimes, though, the other bird notices the cowbird's egg. Different birds respond in different ways. Some push the cowbird's egg out of the nest. Others build a new nest on top of the old nest. Some even eat the cowbird's egg.

Write About Write a paragraph about a trick someone played on you. Then circle each action verb in your sentences.

_____
_____
_____
_____
_____
_____
_____
_____
_____

Review Listen to each word. Circle **VERB** if it is an action verb. Circle **NOT A VERB** if it is not an action verb.

1. VERB   NOT A VERB
2. VERB   NOT A VERB
3. VERB   NOT A VERB
4. VERB   NOT A VERB
5. VERB   NOT A VERB
6. VERB   NOT A VERB
7. VERB   NOT A VERB
8. VERB   NOT A VERB

© The Continental Press, Inc.   DUPLICATING THIS MATERIAL IS ILLEGAL.

Lesson 2: Direct Objects

Remember A **direct object** is a noun or pronoun that receives the action of an action verb. A compound direct object uses a conjunction. The direct object answers what or whom after the verb.

The Maya built large stone <u>monuments</u>.

Their cities contained <u>pyramids</u> and <u>palaces</u>.

They also created <u>murals</u>, <u>jewelry</u>, and <u>sculptures</u>.

Think About How is a direct object different from the subject?

_____

_____

Read and Apply Read the sentences. Underline the direct object in each one.

Thick white clouds cloak Venus. They hide it from our view. Clouds did not stop scientists, though. They explored this planet with unmanned spacecraft. Deep under the clouds, the spacecraft performed tests. They measured the temperature. With special instruments, they collected information. Then the spacecraft sent it back to the scientists. Other spacecraft photographed the clouds and the surface. The clouds contain sulfur dioxide and sulfuric acid. In some photographs, you can see two large continents. No seas surround them, however. In fact, Venus has no water at all. The harsh climate of Venus destroyed many spacecraft. The intense heat burned them. The planet's temperature reaches 870 degrees Fahrenheit!

© The Continental Press, Inc. **DUPLICATING THIS MATERIAL IS ILLEGAL.**

Write About Imagine that you are in a spaceship looking down at a new planet you have just discovered. Write a paragraph telling what you see on the planet. Then circle each direct object or compound direct object in your sentences.

_____
_____
_____
_____
_____
_____
_____
_____
_____

Review Underline the direct object in each sentence. If the sentence has a compound direct object, circle the main words.

1. High winds destroyed the old wooden fence.

2. Elena ate salad and soup.

3. Jack read a chapter of the book.

4. Fans entered the stadium.

5. After the show, the cast took off their costumes and wigs.

6. Julia speaks Spanish and a little French.

Lesson 3: Linking and Helping Verbs

Remember A **linking verb** connects the subject of a sentence to words in the predicate. It shows what the noun is or how it appears.

| is | was | seem | taste | look | sounded |
| are | were | appear | smell | feel | became |

A **helping verb** usually comes before the **main verb.** It helps the main verb express the action or show the connection. Together the two verbs form a **verb phrase.**

<u>will</u> go   <u>had</u> looked   <u>was</u> smelling   <u>could</u> ask

Think About How can you tell the difference between a linking verb and a helping verb?

_____

_____

Read and Apply Read the sentences. Circle each linking verb. Underline each helping verb.

Who is the greatest American poet? Many people will name Walt Whitman. This New York native was born in 1819. By 11 years old, he had left school. But he would continue his education in his travels and his many jobs. Whitman's poetry was inspired by his unusual experiences.

In 1855, Whitman's first collection of poems was published. His poems were very different from the other poetry of the day. They seemed strange to many people. No publisher would print the poems. Whitman felt the poems were important, so he would pay to publish them himself. Years later, Whitman would revise the collection. People became interested in his work. Today, people around the world are reading the poems in *Leaves of Grass.*

Write About Write a paragraph about an experience you have had that you think would be a good subject for a poem. Circle each linking verb you use. Underline each helping verb you use.

Review Read each sentence. Look at the underlined word. Write **L** on the line if it is a linking verb. Write **H** if it is a helping verb.

1. This candle <u>smells</u> like apple pie. _____

2. Children <u>are</u> playing on the swings. _____

3. Everything <u>appears</u> normal here. _____

4. Luc <u>became</u> very upset. _____

5. Next week, we <u>will</u> leave for vacation. _____

6. I <u>am</u> finished with my homework. _____

Lesson 4: Simple Future and Present Tense

Remember A verb in **future tense** tells about something that is going to happen. Use the helping verb *will* to make the future tense.

I <u>will complete</u> my painting after dinner.

A verb in **present tense** tells about what is happening now or all the time. Its form changes to agree with the sentence subject. Just the verb is used with a plural subject and with the pronouns *you* and *I*. With a singular subject, a suffix is added to the verb.

Plural Most plants <u>grow</u> best with lots of light. They <u>reach</u> their greatest heights in the sun. They <u>rely</u> on the sun for food.

Singular A mushroom, however, <u>grows</u> in dark rooms. No light <u>reaches</u> it there. It <u>relies</u> on soil for its food.

Think About In present tense, what suffixes are added to make verbs agree with a singular subject? If a verb ends in *s, x, sh, ch,* or *z*, which suffix is used? If the verb ends in a consonant plus *y*, what suffix is used?

_____

_____

Read and Apply Read the sentences. Find the four verbs that are in the incorrect form. Cross out each incorrect verb and write the correct form above it.

Grasslands cover much of Africa, and huge herds grazes on them. Usually one animal acts as a lookout while the others eat. Always alert, the lookout watchs for lions.

With its tawny color, the lion blends into the grass. The grazing animals never see it. Quietly and patiently, the big cat zeroes in on one animal. Suddenly, it rushies toward its prey and knocks it to the ground. But many times the hunter miss, and then all the animals escape.

38

© The Continental Press, Inc. **DUPLICATING THIS MATERIAL IS ILLEGAL.**

Write About Read each sentence. Rewrite each one with the helping verb *will* to make it tell about the future.

1. Lionesses work as a team to hunt for food.
   _____

2. At night, they find antelope or zebra.
   _____

3. The male lions eat the meat first.
   _____

4. The pride of lions rests during the day.
   _____

5. A lion sleeps from 16 to 20 hours a day.
   _____

Review Read each sentence. Write **F** on the line if the sentence is in future tense. Write **P** on the line if it is in present tense.

1. Only humans hunt lions.   _____

2. Some groups work to protect lions.   _____

3. The number of lions will go down.   _____

Write the correct form of the verb that is under each line.

4. Lions _____ about 13 years.
          live

5. The male leader _____ the young males out of the pride.
                    push

6. A lioness _____ her prey in the bushes.
              spy

Lesson 5: Simple Past Tense

Remember A verb in the **past tense** tells about what has already happened. The past tense of most verbs is made by adding a suffix.

borrow + ed = borrow<u>ed</u>   wipe + d = wip<u>ed</u>

Sometimes a change must be made in the root word.

reply → repl<u>i</u> + ed = repl<u>ied</u>

If a verb ends in consonant-vowel-consonant, the final consonant is usually doubled when the suffix *ed* is added.

jog → jog<u>g</u> + ed = jog<u>ged</u>   glow → glow + ed = glow<u>ed</u>

Think About Summarize the rules for making verbs past tense.

_____

_____

Read and Apply Read the sentences. Find the six incorrect past-tense verb forms. Cross out each one and write the correct verb form above it.

Every day, Mary McLeod Bethune walked five miles to school. She valueed education. In the evenings, Mary shared what she learned with her family. Mary attended college and planed to teach. In 1904, she started a school for African American children. She woried about the children's future. The young teacher struggled to find the money for her school. She askked strangers for money. She showwed wealthy patrons how an education helped the children. Soon the school expanded. Mary's students studied hard. Mary knew they deserved a good education.

Write About Write a paragraph about something that you were afraid to do at first, but that you got up the courage to do.

_____
_____
_____
_____
_____
_____
_____
_____
_____

Review Write the past tense of the verb that is under each line.

1. A fox _____ a lizard among the rocks.
   trap

2. The mechanic _____ the car.
   fix

3. I _____ the box upstairs.
   carry

4. The doctor _____ to my heartbeat.
   listen

5. My little sister _____ her teddy bear.
   cuddle

Lesson 6: Simple Past Tense: Irregular Forms

Remember The past tense of some verbs is made by changing their spelling.

Present	feed	have	go	eat	sell	find	spend	buy
Past	fed	had	went	ate	sold	found	spent	bought

Some verbs do not change at all.

Present	cut	hit	spread
Past	cut	hit	spread

Think About You know that the past tenses of verbs are made in different ways. How can you find out how a verb changes?

_____

_____

Read and Apply Read the sentences. Find the five incorrect past-tense verb forms. Cross out each one and write the correct verb form above it.

On September 25, 1981, Sandra Day O'Connor maked history. She became the first woman on the US Supreme Court. On that day, she putted on her black robe and took her oath of office.

Sandra Day O'Connor came from Arizona. She was a lawyer, and she understood government. So, in 1972, she run for the state senate. She won easily because people knowed she was honest. Then her career in government began. Nine years later, Sandra Day O'Connor met President Ronald Reagan. He think she would make a good Supreme Court justice. So he gave her this important position.

42

© The Continental Press, Inc.   DUPLICATING THIS MATERIAL IS ILLEGAL.

Write About

Write a paragraph about someone you know who is good at something. Tell how that person became good at it.

_____
_____
_____
_____
_____
_____
_____
_____
_____
_____

Review

Write the past tense of the verb that is under each line. Use a dictionary if you need help.

1. The snake _____ its skin.
   shed

2. Farmers _____ corn, beans, and wheat.
   grow

3. I could not buy ice cream because I _____ all my money.
   spend

4. Lacey _____ her diary in a locked box.
   keep

5. The balloon _____ and scared me.
   burst

6. Mom and Dad _____ many things at the yard sale.
   sell

Lesson 7

Progressive Tense

Remember To write in **progressive tense,** use a helping verb and the **present participle** of the verb. The present participle is made by adding *ing* to a verb. For past progressive tense, use the past tense of the helping verb. For present progressive tense, use the present tense of the helping verb. For future progressive tense, use the word *will* with the helping verb.

Past Progressive	I was eating an apple.	The stars were shining.
Present Progressive	I am eating an apple.	The stars are shining.
Future Progressive	I will be eating an apple.	The stars will be shining.

Think About How can you tell if the progressive tense is past, present, or future?

_____

_____

Read and Apply Read the sentences. There are five mistakes with helping verbs or present participles. Circle the incorrect words.

It was World War I. A huge ship were waiting on the airfield. Its engines were huming, and soon soldiers were boarding the ship. Finally, they were throwing off the lines that held it down, and the ship was rissing. Now the pilot was guiding it toward the coast. Soon the ship was skimming the waves. The soldiers was looking for submarines below. They were planning to attack the submarines. Today, however, people were riding airships, or blimps as they are now called, for more peaceful purposes.

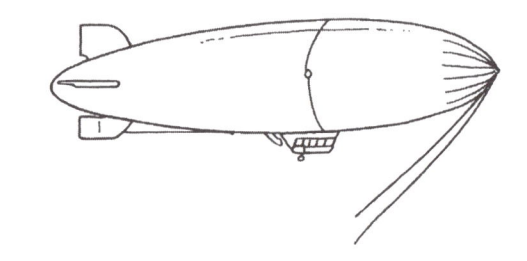

44

© The Continental Press, Inc. **DUPLICATING THIS MATERIAL IS ILLEGAL.**

Write About

Look back at the paragraph in Read and Apply. Rewrite the five sentences that have mistakes. Use the correct helping verb or present participle.

_____
_____
_____
_____
_____
_____
_____
_____
_____

Review

Read the sentences. Write the correct helping verb and present participle of the given verb on the line to complete each sentence.

1. I _____ to go to the water park tomorrow.
   hope

2. It _____ during the entire football game.
   rain

3. When we go to Boston, we _____ Old North Church.
   visit

4. The men _____ the basement of the house yesterday.
   dig

5. Mr. Chen _____ the team next season.
   coach

6. The girls _____ flags in the parade.
   carry

© The Continental Press, Inc.   DUPLICATING THIS MATERIAL IS ILLEGAL.

Lesson 8: Perfect Tense

Remember To write in **perfect tense,** use the helping verbs *have, has,* and *had* with the **past participle** of the main verb. For most verbs, the past participle is the same as the past tense. The helping verb and the past participle make a **verb phrase.**

Past Perfect Tense	had tried	had shut
Present Perfect Tense	has hoped	have asked
Future Perfect Tense	will have stopped	will have brought

Think About Look at the examples above. What does each verb phrase contain?

_____

_____

Read and Apply Read the sentences. There are five incorrect past participles. Cross out the incorrect word and write the correct word above it.

In Japan, people of all ages have practiced the art of origami for hundreds of years. Men, women, and children have foldded square pieces of paper carefully. They have not make any cuts or tears. They have created beautiful figures, such as animals, flowers, and people.

For a long time, people have believed that an origami paper crane has special power. Stories have tell how people who folded 1,000 paper cranes were granted a wish. Now, it has starts to stand for peace, too. A little girl named Sadako had developed a disease because of a bomb. She had tryed to fold 1,000 cranes so her wish to get better would come true. Even though Sadako has died, her dream for peace in the world has lived on.

Write About

Write five sentences in perfect tense. Use some of the verbs in the box. Do not use any verb twice.

| belong | work | buy | pay | win | sleep |
| clap | amaze | prop | laugh | tell | grab |

1. _____
   _____
2. _____
   _____
3. _____
   _____
4. _____
   _____
5. _____
   _____

Review

In each sentence, write the past participle form of a verb. Then write *past*, *present*, or *future* on the line to tell when the action is happening.

1. The woman had _____ the camera.   _____
                        lift

2. Angel has _____ for his watch.   _____
                look

3. The goats had _____ over the buckets.   _____
                   knock

4. By tomorrow, we will have _____ this puzzle.   _____
                                     complete

Lesson 9: Perfect Tense with Irregular Past Participles

Remember **Perfect tense** uses the helping verbs *have, has,* and *had* with the **past participle** of the main verb. Some verbs have irregular past participles.

Present	go	do	give	ride	see	know	rise	speak
Past	went	did	gave	rode	saw	knew	rose	spoke
Past Participle	gone	done	given	ridden	seen	known	risen	spoken

Think About How are the past participles shown above different from other past participles?

_____

_____

Read and Apply Read the sentences. There are five incorrect helping verbs or past participles. Cross out the incorrect word and write the correct word above it. Use a dictionary if you need help.

In the distance, the mast of a ship has rose above the horizon. Every sailor has seen the mast appear before the ship itself. Since ancient times, sailors have knew that this happens because the earth is round. This fact had given them the confidence to explore when other people thought the world was flat.

The ancient Phoenicians were traders who has done a lot of sailing. By 1500 BC, their sailors had went all over the Mediterranean Sea. They had ridden the swift currents of the Atlantic Ocean.

Over 2,000 years later, Viking explorers did the same thing. They had spoken about a strange country far across the ocean. There is proof that the Vikings had saw America 500 years before Columbus did.

Write About Write five sentences in perfect tense. Use some of the verbs in the box. Do not use any verb twice. Use a dictionary if you need help.

| begin | wake | shake | forget | throw |
| speak | choose | draw | freeze | ring |

1. _____

2. _____

3. _____

4. _____

5. _____

Review Complete each sentence by writing the past participle form of the verb.

1. After we have _____ dinner, we will go to the movie.
   eat

2. Jameson has _____ six miles already.
   run

3. I had _____ my name on my homework.
   write

4. The cat had _____ a hole in the curtain.
   tear

5. Someone has _____ my wallet!
   steal

© The Continental Press, Inc. DUPLICATING THIS MATERIAL IS ILLEGAL.

UNIT 4: Pronouns
Lesson 1: Subject and Object Pronouns

Remember A **pronoun** is a word that takes the place of a noun. A pronoun refers to a certain noun, which is called the **referent.** A **subject pronoun** is used in the subject part of a sentence.

Singular	I	you	he	she	it
Plural	we	you	they		

An **object pronoun** is used after an action verb and after such words as *at, by, in, from, for,* and *with.*

Singular	me	you	him	her	it
Plural	us	you	them		

Think About Which subject and object pronouns can take the place of nouns that name people? Which can take the place of nouns that name animals, places, or things?

_____

_____

Read and Apply Read the sentences. Underline each subject pronoun. Circle each object pronoun.

We can thank Scott Joplin for giving us ragtime music. This black composer wrote some of the most famous rags, or songs. He sang and played piano, guitar, and cornet. He published "The Maple Leaf Rag" in 1899. It became the best-selling ragtime song ever. Joplin wrote more rags and performed them around the country.

Rags have a lively beat in them. They make you want to dance. After Joplin died in 1916, many people forgot about him and his music. However, ragtime became popular again. Today, people enjoy listening to it. It is considered a completely American style of music. Would you like to hear a rag?

© The Continental Press, Inc.   DUPLICATING THIS MATERIAL IS ILLEGAL.

Write About Write a paragraph about a type of music that you enjoy. Tell about a musician or singer who performs this type of music. Underline each subject pronoun. Circle each object pronoun.

_____
_____
_____
_____
_____
_____
_____
_____
_____

Review Complete each sentence by writing a pronoun in the blank. Underline the referent.

1. Derrick laughed after _____ told the joke.

2. Anya washed the car, and then she waxed _____.

3. Micah asked Mom, "Do _____ know where my coat is?"

4. People often forget where _____ parked their cars.

5. Hope thinks _____ will come to the party.

6. I texted Lydia to tell _____ the news.

Lesson 2: Possessive Pronouns

Remember A **possessive pronoun** tells who or what has something. It shows ownership. Some possessive pronouns come before a noun. Others are used alone.

Before Nouns	my	your	his	her	its	our	their
Alone	mine	yours	his	hers	its	ours	theirs

<u>My</u> brother lost <u>his</u> favorite hat.

I know where <u>mine</u> is. Do you know where <u>yours</u> is?

Think About Look at the examples. Which pronouns can be used both ways?

_____

Read and Apply Read the sentences. Underline the possessive pronouns.

Today, Mrs. Stein took her class on a fossil hunt. The class decided the trip was its favorite of the whole year. The students got to wear their oldest clothes.

Everyone found fossils. Dan showed his to Mrs. Stein. He asked, "Is my fossil a dinosaur bone?"

His teacher looked at Dan's fossil carefully. "No, yours is a little sea creature," she explained to him.

"What kind of fossil is mine?" Jill wondered as she gave hers to Mrs. Stein.

"Your rock has a fossil leaf printed on it," the teacher said.

"Our class found lots of fossils today," Dan said to Jill. "The best display in the school will be ours."

Write About Write a sentence using each pronoun correctly.

1. yours
   _____

2. their
   _____

3. hers
   _____

4. my
   _____

5. ours
   _____

6. mine
   _____

Review Read the sentences. Above each underlined phrase, write a possessive pronoun to take its place.

1. Leon, my pencil is broken, can I borrow <u>Leon's pencil</u>?

2. Amber found <u>Amber's</u> shoe under the bed.

3. Mr. and Mrs. Bradley sold <u>Mr. and Mrs. Bradley's</u> house.

4. My sister and I pitched <u>my sister's and my</u> tent in the backyard.

5. The picture on the right is <u>my picture</u>.

6. The dog buried <u>the dog's</u> bone under the tree.

Lesson 3: Relative Pronouns

Remember A **relative pronoun** refers back to a noun earlier in the sentence. It introduces a clause that either identifies the noun or it gives more information about the noun. There are five relative pronouns in English.

that	which	who	whom	whose

The man who bought the car drove it away.

The clause *who bought the car* identifies the man.

I took the cookies, which were now burnt, out of the oven.

The clause *which were now burnt* gives more information about the cookies.

Think About What is the job of a relative pronoun?

Read and Apply Read the sentences. Put a line under each relative pronoun. Circle the noun that it refers to in the sentence.

Ferdinand Magellan was a Portuguese explorer who led the first European voyage around the world. Magellan sailed in several voyages that went to East Africa, Malaysia, and Morocco. Eventually, Magellan had a disagreement with the Portuguese king, who then refused to send him on any more voyages. Magellan asked the king of Spain, whose grandparents had sent Christopher Columbus on his explorations, to give him money for another voyage.

In 1519, Magellan set sail with five ships that were loaded with men and supplies. Across the Atlantic Ocean, he discovered a narrow waterway, which is now known as the Magellan Strait. In the Philippines, Magellan met a native king with whom he developed a friendship. Magellan was killed in a battle there. Only one of the five ships that started the voyage returned to Spain.

Write About Use each of the relative pronouns listed in a sentence.

1. who
   _____
   _____

2. whom
   _____
   _____

3. that
   _____
   _____

4. whose
   _____
   _____

5. which
   _____
   _____

Review Write a relative pronoun in each blank to complete the sentences.

1. The girl _____ name I cannot remember is in front of me.

2. The doctor _____ you are seeing is ready.

3. My aunt's house, _____ is very old, has a big fireplace.

4. We waited for Jeremy, _____ was running late.

5. Kym found a book _____ was on the wrong shelf.

Lesson 4: Self-Pronouns

Remember A *self*-pronoun refers back to the subject of the sentence. It must agree with the subject.

Singular	myself	yourself	himself	herself	itself
Plural	ourselves	yourselves	themselves		

I won a trip for a friend and <u>myself</u>.

Mom said we could not go by <u>ourselves</u>.

Think About How are singular *self*-pronouns different from plural ones?

_____

_____

Read and Apply Read the sentences. Underline the *self*-pronouns. Circle the incorrect *self*-pronoun.

Anton van Leeuwenhoek never received a formal education himself, but he made major contributions to science. Van Leeuwenhoek used a small magnifying glass for the first time when he was 16 years old. The magnifying glass itself fascinated him and he soon began creating his own. He created several usable microscopes and used them to study the tiny organisms in nature for himself. He also studied blood cells and bacteria.

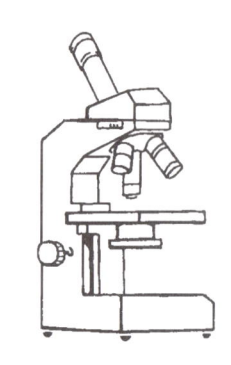

Van Leeuwenhoek wrote letters to important scientists so they could read for ourselves the interesting discoveries he was making. Word spread about van Leeuwenhoek's discoveries and people wanted to see his microscopes for themselves. The queen of England even visited him so that she could look through a microscope for herself! Today, our microscopes are much different than what van Leeuwenhoek created. But his work allows you to see for yourself the tiny details of life.

Write About

Write about something you would like to look at underneath a microscope. What do you think you would see? Use at least two *self*-pronouns.

_____
_____
_____
_____
_____
_____
_____
_____
_____

Review

Fill in the circle next to each sentence in which the correct *self*-pronoun is used. If the *self*-pronoun is incorrect, cross it out and write the correct pronoun on the line.

○ Place the vase on the shelf by itself.   _____

○ We found out for themselves that we were wrong.   _____

○ The king himself visited the city.   _____

○ You have to see this for yourself!   _____

○ Zoe soon found myself hopelessly lost.   _____

○ "Can you make lunch by yourself?" Mom asked us.   _____

○ Someday I want to see Paris for herself.   _____

○ The people seated themselves on the grass.   _____

57

Lesson 1

UNIT 5: Adjectives and Adverbs
Adjectives and Articles

Remember An **adjective** is a word that describes a noun or pronoun. It tells what kind, how many, or which one.

<u>Brown</u> seaweed floated on the <u>calm</u> sea.

The <u>sandy</u> beach was <u>empty</u>.

An **article** is a special kind of adjective. Its only job is to signal that a noun will follow. There are three articles: *a, an,* and *the*.

<u>The</u> wind blew <u>an</u> apple off <u>a</u> tree.

Think About Look at the examples. What is different about where the adjectives are in a sentence and where the articles are in the sentence? Where does an article always come?

_____

_____

Read and Apply Read the sentences. Underline each adjective or article. Draw an arrow from each adjective to the noun or pronoun that it describes. Draw an arrow from each article to the noun or pronoun that it signals.

The pyramids of Egypt are huge. They are the graves of ancient pharaohs. Their construction was hard, dirty work. It was difficult, and it took many years. Each pyramid was made out of enormous blocks of stone. Hundreds of strong workers used thick ropes to move the stones.

Inside a pyramid are burial chambers. A pharaoh filled his massive pyramid with beautiful paintings, gold pots, and magnificent furniture. Dangerous traps protected the great riches. But clever thieves have stolen many things as the years have passed.

58

© The Continental Press, Inc.   **DUPLICATING THIS MATERIAL IS ILLEGAL.**

Write About

Write about something in a different country that you would like to see someday. Describe what it is and why you want to see it.

_____
_____
_____
_____
_____
_____
_____
_____
_____

Review

Complete each sentence by filling in the blank with either an adjective or an article.

1. _____ _____ duck swam on the pond.
   article   adjective

2. _____ buildings were _____ and _____.
   article   adjective   adjective

3. We played _____ _____ game.
              article   adjective

4. Grandma baked _____ _____ cookies.
                   adjective   adjective

Lesson 2: Comparing with Adjectives

Remember For most short adjectives, suffixes are used to make comparing forms. **Comparative** adjectives compare two nouns. Add *er* to make a comparative form. **Superlative** adjectives compare more than two. Add *est* to make a superlative form.

Comparative The castle was older than the church.
Superlative The bridge was the oldest bridge in the country.

Sometimes the root word must be changed when a suffix is added.

pretty → pretti + er = prettier   pretti + est = prettiest
wide → wid + er = wider   wid + est = widest
hot → hott + er = hotter   hott + est = hottest

Think About How do the adjectives show how many nouns are being compared?

___

Read and Apply Read the sentences. Find six adjectives that are written incorrectly. Cross out each one and write the correct form above it.

George Herriman was one of the fineest comic strip artist who ever lived. But we have fewwer facts about him than about most cartoonists.

Krazy Kat was Herriman's funniest strip. It was about the sillier cat and the meanest mouse in the world. The mouse throws bricks at the cat, who loves the mouse. Every brick is larger than the last. But that just makes the cat happyer than before and the mouse madder than ever!

In 1913, *Krazy Kat* was the newest strip in the comics. It was not the biggest hit of its time, but it had a longest run than many comics. Many people still think it was one of the greattest comics of all time.

Write About Write a paragraph comparing two different comic strips or cartoons.

_____
_____
_____
_____
_____
_____
_____
_____
_____
_____

Review Read the sentences. Write the correct comparing form of the adjective that is under each line.

1. This stamp is the _____ in my collection.
   rare

2. Draw a _____ line below the first one.
   thin

3. This house has the _____ yard decorations on the block.
   crazy

4. The steak knife is _____ than the butter knife.
   sharp

5. Keira is a _____ runner than Liz.
   swift

6. The _____ cat ate all the food.
   greedy

Lesson 3: More Comparing with Adjectives

Remember The comparing forms of longer adjectives are made by using the words *more, most, less,* or *least* before the adjective. Some adjectives have special comparing forms.

Adjective	difficult	loyal	good	bad
Comparative	more difficult	less loyal	better	worse
Superlative	most difficult	least loyal	best	worst

Think About Look at the first two columns of examples. How are the words *more, most, less,* and *least* used?

_____

_____

Read and Apply Read the sentences. There are five mistakes with the words *more, most, less,* and *least.* Cross out each incorrect word and write the correct word above it.

Samurais were the most courageous and most disciplined warriors in Japan. The best warriors were some of the more powerful people in the country. These men trained in swords, longbows, and other weapons. People feared even the less skilled fighter. A samurai's sword was the most important thing he owned. He believed that it held his soul.

The samurais worked for local rulers in Japan. Many people were least devoted to these leaders than samurais. Samurais held themselves to a most strict code of behavior than others. They believed in honor, bravery, obedience, and self-sacrifice. The more meaningful part of being a samurai—the code of honor—still exists in much of Japanese society.

Write About Write a paragraph about what you think it was like to be a samurai. Use at least one comparative and one superlative adjective.

_____
_____
_____
_____
_____
_____
_____
_____
_____
_____

Review Circle the correct word to complete each sentence.

1. The [better   best] workout uses all of your muscles.

2. Juanita is [more   most] timid than Amid.

3. Seth was the [less   least] mature in the group.

4. This turn is the [more   most] dangerous part of the road.

5. These cookies taste [worse   worst] than the other ones.

6. I'm glad this campsite is [less   least] primitive than the last one.

© The Continental Press, Inc. **DUPLICATING THIS MATERIAL IS ILLEGAL.**

Lesson 4: Order of Adjectives

Remember When you use more than one adjective to describe a noun, follow the correct order for the adjectives.

1. Opinion 2. Size and Shape 3. Age 4. Color and Pattern 5. Origin 6. Material

I found a gorgeous, round, antique, purple Venetian glass bead.
[opinion, shape, age, color, origin, material]

This TV show is about a silly, big, orange bird. [opinion, size, color]

I received a new striped wool sweater for my birthday.
[age, pattern, material]

Put the beautiful, soft, blue blanket on your bed. [opinion, opinion, color]

Think About Try writing or saying one of the examples above with the adjectives in a different order. How does it sound to you?

Read and Apply Read the sentences. Underline the group of adjectives that is in the incorrect order.

It wasn't until halfway through the terrible long American Civil War that African Americans were allowed to fight. A group of African American men gathered in Massachusetts and formed the first all-black Union regiment. A courageous, white dedicated, young officer named Robert Shaw led them.

At first, the leaders gave the regiment unimportant, small things to do in the war. Then Shaw asked to lead the next Union charge. On July 18, 1863, the regiment gathered on the narrow, dark, sandy beach near Fort Wagner in South Carolina. They charged toward the strong, tall stone walls of the Southern fort with Shaw in the lead. Many of the brave young African American Union soldiers died that day. Shaw led the attack and died with them. Even though they lost the battle, the regiment made a place for itself in history.

© The Continental Press, Inc. **DUPLICATING THIS MATERIAL IS ILLEGAL.**

Write About Write five sentences. Use the types of adjectives listed for each sentence.

1. [opinion, shape, material]

   _____

   _____

2. [size, age, color, origin]

   _____

   _____

3. [opinion, opinion, age]

   _____

   _____

4. [shape, pattern, origin, material]

   _____

   _____

5. [size, shape, color, pattern]

   _____

   _____

Review Fill in the circle next to each sentence that shows adjectives in the correct order.

- ○ The shop sold white, lovely, lace, antique Irish tablecloths.
- ○ An ugly, old, gray dog barked in the yard.
- ○ Jim found a large, round, blue, striped glass marble on the floor.
- ○ A black, tiny, gross bug landed on my hand.
- ○ We looked at the new, interesting, granite Italian sculpture.

© The Continental Press, Inc. DUPLICATING THIS MATERIAL IS ILLEGAL.

Lesson 5: Adverbs

Remember An **adverb** is a word that describes a verb. It tells how, when, or where the action happened.

- **How** Eric wrestles <u>well</u>.
- **When** <u>Yesterday</u>, he pinned his opponent in 15 seconds.
- **Where** Eric can take care of himself <u>anywhere</u>.

An adverb can also describe an adjective or another adverb.

- **Adjective** Good campers are <u>always</u> careful.
- **Adverb** Fires can spread <u>very</u> quickly.

Think About Look at the second set of examples. What does *always* tell about *careful*? What does *very* tell about *quickly*?

_____

_____

Read and Apply Read the sentences. Underline each adverb. Then draw an arrow from the adverb to the word it describes.

The Baga people of Guinea have lived quietly on the coast of Africa for hundreds of years. The Baga often worshipped very ancient spirits. One spirit almost always takes a python's shape. The spirit python is a truly gigantic snake. It is so big that when it moves it cuts extremely deep channels into the marsh.

The Baga are widely known for their skillfully carved wooden figures. The people often wore these figures as masks in ceremonies. The great mask usually stands over six feet tall. Today the ceremonies are rarely seen as Baga people slowly move into a contemporary culture.

© The Continental Press, Inc. **DUPLICATING THIS MATERIAL IS ILLEGAL.**

Write About Write sentences using adverbs in the way given.

1. an adverb to describe an action

   _____
   _____

2. an adverb to describe an adjective

   _____
   _____

3. an adverb to describe another adverb

   _____
   _____

4. an adverb to describe an action

   _____
   _____

Review Read each sentence. Write *how, when,* or *where* on the line to tell what information the underlined adverb gives.

1. Olivia never thought she would win the contest. _____

2. The crowd at the concert cheered wildly. _____

3. It is always important to use good manners. _____

4. Avery brings her bike indoors when it rains. _____

5. Very slowly, Ian got into the water. _____

6. I usually enjoy running in the park. _____

Lesson 6: Comparing with Adverbs

Remember An adverb can be used to compare verbs. The **comparative** form compares two. The **superlative** form compares more than two. The comparing forms are made in the same way as the comparing forms of adjectives.

Adverb	high	proudly	slowly
Comparative	high**er**	**more** proudly	**less** slowly
Superlative	high**est**	**most** proudly	**least** slowly

Some adverbs have special comparing forms.

Adverb	well	badly
Comparative	better	worse
Superlative	best	worst

Think About If an adverb ends in *ly*, how are the comparing forms made?

_____

_____

Read and Apply Read the sentences. Circle the correct comparing form for each set.

Today, hard-of-hearing people live [more normally   most normally] than ever before. They use many helpful inventions. Flashing lights wake them [sooner   soonest] than alarm clocks. TV shows and movies are [more easily   most easily] understood when the words are on the screen. And hearing aids are used the [more frequently   most frequently] of all.

One company is working [harder   hardest] than others to improve life for people who have trouble hearing. This company created a hearing aid that recharges using solar power. The batteries last [longer   longest] than regular batteries. They are thrown away [less often   least often]. This technology helps many people hear [better   best]. It is also good for the environment!

Write About Do you know someone who has trouble hearing? Tell what you can do to help that person communicate more easily.

_____
_____
_____
_____
_____
_____
_____
_____
_____

Review Read the sentences. Write the correct comparing form of the adverb that is under each line.

1. I like soccer _____ than basketball.
                          well

2. This speaker sounds _____ than the rest.
                               loud

3. The toddler behaved _____ of all.
                               badly

4. Please handle this crystal vase the _____.
                                                carefully

5. We must feed our dog _____ than the fish.
                                   regularly

© The Continental Press, Inc. **DUPLICATING THIS MATERIAL IS ILLEGAL.**

Lesson 1

UNIT 6: Phrases, Clauses, and Complex Sentences
Prepositional Phrases

Remember An **object of a preposition** is the noun or pronoun that follows a preposition. The **preposition,** its object, and all of the words that come between them form a **prepositional phrase.**

preposition ↓   ↓ object of the preposition
The woman in the white dress arrived on Monday.
preposition ↑   ↑ object of the preposition

Think About Look at the two prepositional phrases above. What is the fewest number of words that are needed to make up a prepositional phrase? What kinds of words are they?

_____

_____

Read and Apply Read the sentences. Underline each prepositional phrase. Circle the object of the preposition.

The world's most famous tortoises live in the Galápagos Islands. These islands are located off South America. Once thousands of giant tortoises made their homes here. No people lived on the islands, but after 1535, ships from Spain began stopping there. The huge animals were hunted for food. In time, few were left.

Scientists around the world were concerned about the tortoises. By 1959, the islands had been turned into a national park. But rats and pigs still ate the tortoises' eggs. Then islanders who lived near the park began protecting the eggs. Still, several types of the tortoises have completely died out. Scientists continue to work to save these interesting reptiles from extinction.

Write About Do wild birds or other animals live near your home? Tell about them and what you can do to help them. Then circle each prepositional phrase in your sentences.

_____
_____
_____
_____
_____
_____
_____
_____

Review Read each sentence. Circle the preposition. Then underline the prepositional phrase. Some sentences have more than one prepositional phrase.

1. I do not like when people talk during a movie.

2. The fence around the yard needs repaired.

3. Before noon, please take the dog for a short walk.

4. Put all the food except the apples in the refrigerator.

5. Mason found a dollar bill on his dresser.

6. There were crumbs on the counter and under the table.

© The Continental Press, Inc. **DUPLICATING THIS MATERIAL IS ILLEGAL.**

Lesson 2: Independent and Dependent Clauses

Remember A **clause** is a group of words that acts together in a sentence. It always has a subject and a predicate. An **independent clause** makes sense by itself. A **dependent clause** does not make sense without the rest of the sentence.

Elliot fell off his bike when he hit a big hole in the ground.

independent clause ↑   ↑ dependent clause

Think About How do you know if a clause is independent or dependent?

_____

_____

Read and Apply Read the sentences. Look at each underlined clause. Write **IND** above it if it is an independent clause. Write **DEP** above it if it is a dependent clause.

John Joseph Merlin lived in London and Paris, where he invented many mechanical creations. After he moved to London in 1760, he opened a museum to display his inventions. Merlin made the first pair of roller skates, which he wore to advertise his museum. His skates each had a single row of small metal wheels, but they did not have brakes. Even though he had invented them, Merlin was not very good at using the roller skates. Merlin wore his new skates to a party where he crashed into a large mirror. Merlin never figured out a good way to stop on his skates so his design never became popular. Years later, other people would create better designs, which led to the modern roller skate.

Write About Write a paragraph about something you would like to invent. Underline and label two independent clauses and one dependent clause.

_____
_____
_____
_____
_____
_____
_____
_____
_____

Review Read each sentence. Put one line under the independent clause. Put two lines under the dependent clause.

1. If it is not raining, I will walk home from school.

2. Curt put on his coat after he put on his boots.

3. Adanya read a magazine while she waited for the dentist.

4. Eat breakfast before you go to school.

5. Since the store had a sale, Emma decided to buy new shoes.

6. I spoke with Ms. Sanchez, who teaches at my school.

Lesson 3: Complex Sentences

Remember A **complex sentence** has one independent clause and at least one dependent clause.

The campers made a campfire <u>after they set up their tents</u>.

<u>When it was burning brightly</u>, some of them cooked dinner <u>while others looked for more firewood</u>.

Tristan, <u>who liked to cook</u>, made burgers <u>that everyone enjoyed</u>.

Think About Where can dependent clauses be located in a complex sentence?

_____

_____

_____

Read and Apply Read the sentences. Underline the complex sentences.

Pompeii was a popular vacation place for ancient Romans until it was completely destroyed by a volcano eruption. The city was close to Mount Vesuvius, and it often experienced earthquakes because of the volcano. The ancient Romans did not realize that earthquakes could be a warning for an eruption. On August 24, 79 AD, Mount Vesuvius erupted. It covered the city of Pompeii in ash before the people had time to get out.

When archaeologists were working in the area hundreds of years later, they found the remains of the city. The ash completely preserved the city. The archaeologists found remains of people just as they had been when the eruption happened. Today, people visit the site of Pompeii, where they can see what life was like in the ancient city.

Write About

Write a paragraph about what you think life might have been like in ancient Pompeii. Use at least two complex sentences. Underline them.

_____
_____
_____
_____
_____
_____
_____
_____

Review

Read the sentences. Fill in the circle next to each complex sentence.

○ In Paris, many people visit the Eiffel Tower.

○ My class eats lunch before we go out to recess.

○ Abby, who loves to play golf, explained the game to me.

○ The soccer team plays on the lower field.

○ Sit down after you get a drink.

○ Since we arrived early, we were first in line.

○ The train pulled into the station, and the people got off.

Lesson 4: Misplaced Modifiers

Remember A **modifier** is a word or group of words that adds detail to a sentence. Adjectives, adverbs, and prepositional phrases are all modifiers.

A <u>small</u> crab <u>quickly</u> ran <u>into the ocean</u>.

The adjective *small* modifies *crab*. The adverb *quickly* and the prepositional phrase *into the ocean* modify *ran*.

Modifiers should be placed close to the word that they describe. Otherwise they can cause confusion. A **misplaced modifier** occurs when the subject of the modifier is unclear because of poor placement in the sentence.

No   The students had a bake sale <u>in the band</u>.

Yes   The students <u>in the band</u> had a bake sale.

Think About Where should modifiers be in a sentence?

_____

_____

Read and Apply Read the sentences. Circle the misplaced modifiers.

From Puerto Rico, Roberto Clemente was a baseball player. He began his major-league career in 1955 and showed his talent for the game quickly. This skillful outfielder for the Pittsburgh Pirates set many records over the years. He was a strong batter and an excellent fielder.

When he was not playing baseball, Clemente helped many people. He eagerly spoke out about civil rights. In 1972, a major earthquake hit Nicaragua. For the victims Clemente gathered supplies immediately. Then, into the Atlantic Ocean, the small plane carrying Clemente and the supplies crashed. Clemente died at age 37. People mourned his sudden death around the world. The sports star was in 1973 elected to the Baseball Hall of Fame.

Write About Read each sentence. Rewrite the sentence and correct the misplaced modifier.

1. Liev laughed at the clowns loudly.
   _____

2. Cora asked the girl a question in the blue coat.
   _____

3. Carefully, Mom packed the breakable dishes.
   _____

4. Mark watched a bird eat through his window.
   _____

5. By the front door, the dog sits.
   _____

Review Read the sentences. Underline the modifiers. Use the lines below to correctly rewrite the two sentences with misplaced modifiers.

1. Gracefully my sister dances on the stage.

2. A brown horse ran through the woods.

3. Hyo with his foot shut the door.

4. We usually ride our bikes to the beach.

5. After breakfast, Mom washed the dirty dishes.

_____

_____

UNIT 7: Capital Letters
Beginning a Sentence or a Direct Quotation

Remember The first word of a sentence begins with a capital letter. The pronoun *I* is always written with a capital letter, too.

Last week, I heard Manuel play the guitar.

A **direct quotation** is the exact words that someone said. In written conversation, begin the first word of a direct quotation with a capital letter.

"Have you read this new book?" asked Jaime.

Marta said, "Is it good?"

Think About If a quotation starts after the beginning of the sentence, is the first word still capitalized? Why?

_____

_____

Read and Apply Read the sentences. Circle each word that should be capitalized.

my class is learning about the Mariana Trench. i told my friend Lily about it.

"what is the Mariana Trench?" asked Lily.

"it's a large canyon on the ocean floor," i explained. i added, "it's about seven miles deep."

Lily said, "that's six miles deeper than the Grand Canyon!" she continued, "the water pressure must be tremendous!"

then my friend Enzo asked, "can anything live so far down?"

i answered, "sure, lots of things live on the ocean floor. those creatures are so used to the great pressure that they can't even live near the surface."

© The Continental Press, Inc. **DUPLICATING THIS MATERIAL IS ILLEGAL.**

Write About Have a conversation with a friend about someplace you would like to visit. Write the exact words that you said and the exact words that your friend said.

_____
_____
_____
_____
_____
_____
_____
_____
_____
_____

Review Read the sentences. Circle the words that should be capitalized. Put a slash through the letters that are incorrectly capitalized.

1. when Jesse came over, i asked, "Did You bring your Baseball?"

2. Our Teacher said, "everyone needs to sit down."

3. "what time does the movie start?" Wondered Rachel.

4. the Woman said, "may i have a cup of coffee?"

5. "the park is two blocks from here," The man told us.

6. Ashley Stated, "before i ride my bike, I check the tires."

Lesson 2

Proper Nouns and Titles of Respect

Remember A **proper noun** begins with a capital letter. If the proper noun has two or more words, each main word begins with a capital letter. Some people have **titles** in their names. Titles also begin with a capital letter.

Deb	President Carson	Queen Elizabeth of England
Canada	Mount Shasta	Wilson Middle School
Bambi	Monday	Ace Tea and Spice Company

Capitalize **initials,** or letters that stand for names. If an **abbreviation** stands for a proper noun, it begins with a capital letter. In United States Postal Service abbreviations for states, both letters are capitals.

| Avenue = Ave. | Thursday = Thurs. | Doctor = Dr. |
| Arkansas = AR | January = Jan. | George = G. |

Think About When are words like *president, mount,* and *company* capitalized? What should you do when you write these words as abbreviations?

_____
_____
_____

Read and Apply Read the sentences. Circle each word or abbreviation that should be capitalized.

In sept. 1899, guglielmo marconi showed people in the united states of america how his radio worked. He broadcast the america's cup race from the *ss saint paul,* a ship in the atlantic ocean. The young inventor from italy soon set up marconi's wireless telegraphy and signal co. In 1909, marconi won the nobel prize for his work.

By the 1930s, news from maine to california was being reported as it happened. Sports fans knew the moment that bold venture won the kentucky derby. The country even listened as pres. franklin d. roosevelt spoke from the white house.

Write About Write a paragraph comparing hearing news on the radio to getting news from another source.

_____
_____
_____
_____
_____
_____
_____
_____

Review Read the groups of words. Circle the words or abbreviations in each one that should be capitalized.

1. a meeting on fri. aug. 1
2. mail for t. a. robertson
3. snowy weather in dec.
4. a city in nd
5. the office of dr. ray m. lee
6. pollution in l. erie
7. a trip to mex. and the caribbean
8. raining in portland, or
9. an accident on lincoln hwy.
10. terrible smog in l.a., ca

Lesson 3: Titles of Works

Remember The first word, last word, and each main word in the **title** of a work begin with a capital letter. This includes titles of books, stories, poems, reports, magazines, newspapers, movies, plays, TV shows, and songs.

Book	*A Wrinkle in Time*
Poem	"Who Has Seen the Wind?"
Newspaper	*Boston Globe*
Movie	*The Secret Life of Pets*
Song	"Take Me Out to the Ball Game"

Think About What kinds of words in a title are not capitalized?

_____

_____

Read and Apply Read the sentences. Circle each word that should be capitalized.

Each language skill is controlled by a different part of your brain. Using one part, you read everything from "the princess and the pea" to *harry potter and the sorcerer's stone.* You use another part to write a letter to *sports illustrated kids* or to do a puzzle in the *daily tribune.* Thanks to the listening center, you can understand the actors speaking in *romeo and juliet.* If this part is injured, you could still enjoy "the voice" on TV or the movie *the adventures of milo and otis* if it was shown with captions. If the speech center gets hurt, you couldn't recite "paul revere's ride" or "casey at the bat." But you could sing "america the beautiful." That's because music is connected with another part of your brain.

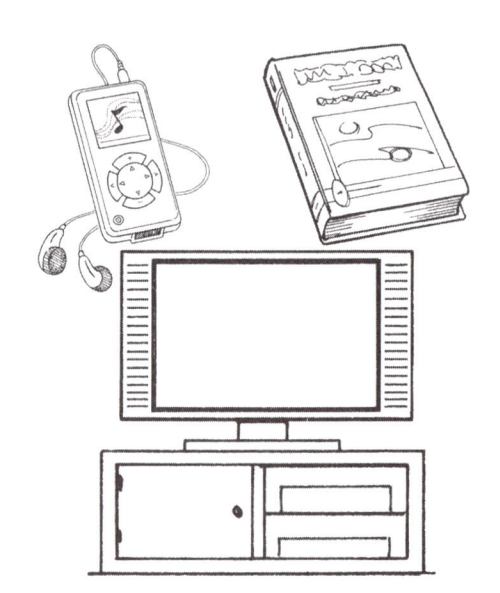

Write About Write each title on the line. Use correct capitalization.

1. Write the title of your favorite book.
   _____

2. Write the title of your favorite TV show.
   _____

3. Write the title of a song you like right now.
   _____

4. Write the title of a movie you saw recently.
   _____

5. Write the title of a play that you have seen or would like to see.
   _____

6. Write the title of a book or a story that you would like to read.
   _____

Review Fill in the circle next to each title that shows correct capitalization. If the title is capitalized incorrectly, circle the words that should be capitalized. Cross out the words that should not be capitalized.

○ *The sound of music*

○ *"mary had a little Lamb"*

○ *National Geographic Kids*

○ *The Jungle Book*

○ *"Wind On The Hill"*

○ *Snow White And the Seven Dwarfs*

○ *Toy Story*

Lesson 1

UNIT 8: Punctuation and Style

End Punctuation and Other Uses of a Period

Remember A **period (.)** ends a declarative or imperative sentence. A **question mark (?)** ends an interrogative sentence. An **exclamation point (!)** ends an exclamatory sentence or an imperative sentence that shows strong feeling.

I love the county fair. Look at those lambs. Have you ever seen anything so cute? What an enormous bull! Don't stand too close!

A period is also used after an **initial** and after many **abbreviations.**

John Fitzgerald Kennedy = J.F.K.   inch = in.
Mister = Mr.   Saturday = Sat.

Think About Look at the abbreviations again. A period is not used after the abbreviation for most measurements. Why would the abbreviation for *inch* be treated differently? What word could it be confused with?

_____

_____

Read and Apply Read the sentences. End each one with the correct punctuation mark.

Can you imagine staying in a hotel under the sea What an amazing sight to see fish outside the window You can live this dream at an underwater lodge in Florida Where exactly is this hotel It is 30 feet under water How do people get down to it First, they have to learn how to scuba dive Watch out for spiny lobsters on the way down Hotel guests can explore the lagoon Be sure that your tanks are filled with air Oh, how beautiful it is down here When you are finished, relax in your room and watch the fish through your window You can even have pizza delivered

© The Continental Press, Inc.   DUPLICATING THIS MATERIAL IS ILLEGAL.

Write About Read the groups of words. Rewrite each group using an initial or an abbreviation for each underlined word. Use a dictionary if you need help.

1. Wednesday, December 25 _____

2. 239 North Mary Street _____

3. Ajax Corporation _____

4. Admiral Lee Baggett _____

5. Martin Luther King, Junior _____

6. Justice Department _____

7. five inches deep _____

8. Governor Madeleine Kunin _____

9. Saint Lawrence River _____

10. Mount Rainier _____

Review Fill in the circle next to each sentence that shows correct use of periods, question marks, and exclamation points. If something is incorrect in the sentence, circle the mistake.

○ When was John Q. Adams president!

○ Turn left on S. Main St. near the train station.

○ Look at Mt. Everest!

○ Where does the Mississippi R. start?

○ On Mon., I visited D.r Kreider.

○ This dept. is in charge of finances?

Lesson 2: Comma

Remember A **comma (,)** is used to separate things. It separates:

- the day from the year in a date and the city from the state or country
  We visited Chicago, Illinois, on July 9, 2017.

- the name of a person being spoken to and words like *yes, no, well,* and *however* from the rest of the sentence
  Carly, I have never tried snowboarding. Ted, however, loves it.

- three or more words or groups of words in a series
  The squirrels run, leap from branches, and climb trees.

- the two parts of a compound sentence
  We enjoyed the ballet, and we met the dancers afterward.

Think About Look at the examples above. What can you decide about the use of a comma?

_____

Read and Apply Read the sentences. Put commas where they belong. Use the proofreading mark shown below.

"Anita how was your trip?"

⌃ add a comma

"Well Kyle we went to San Francisco California. I saw the Golden Gate Bridge Alcatraz Island and Lombard Street. The Golden Gate Bridge was the longest suspension bridge in the world but now 13 bridges are longer than it. Alcatraz Island had a prison on it and many famous prisoners were held there. It closed on March 21 1963. We rode a boat to the island took a tour of the prison and saw the lighthouse."

"Is there something special about Lombard Street Anita?"

"Yes Kyle there is! One block is very steep and it has eight very tight turns."

Write About Write a paragraph telling about an interesting place you have visited. Write as though you are talking to someone. Be sure to use commas correctly.

_____
_____
_____
_____
_____
_____
_____
_____

Review Read the sentences. Put commas where they belong. Circle commas that are in the wrong place.

1. Yes Mineko, you might see a giraffe a lion an elephant, and a zebra, at the zoo.

2. I was born on July 18 2010 in Rochester New, York.

3. We visited Orlando Florida on February 2, 2017 but we did not stay very long.

4. Antonio please, bring the cups plates and napkins, to the table.

5. After June, 7 2018, this museum in Richmond Virginia will be closed.

© The Continental Press, Inc.   DUPLICATING THIS MATERIAL IS ILLEGAL.

Lesson 3: Apostrophe

Remember An **apostrophe (')** is used to take the place of the letter or letters that are left out of a **contraction**.

do not	she is	I will	they would
don't	she's	I'll	they'd

An apostrophe is also used to make a noun possessive.

the cat that Miranda has = Miranda's cat
the father of the twins = the twins' father
a store for men = a men's store

Think About What is a contraction made of?

___

Read and Apply Read the sentences. Above each group of underlined words, write a possessive noun and its object or a contraction to replace it.

Do not try to eat a raw olive. You will find that they taste awful because they are full of strong chemicals. Olives must be soaked in lye or they could not be eaten. Lye is not good to eat by itself, but we are able to eat olives with lye in them. That is because it is changed by the chemicals of the olives.

Olive trees cannot grow everywhere. The climate of the area must be just right. It should not get too cold. Olive trees can live more than 1,000 years. If the nutrients of the soil are right and the tree is not hurt by disease, it will continue to make olives for many years. The trunks of the trees are often short and twisted. The fruit of the tree can be eaten or made into oil.

88

© The Continental Press, Inc.   DUPLICATING THIS MATERIAL IS ILLEGAL.

Write About Write a paragraph about a food you don't like. Give two reasons why you don't like it.

_____
_____
_____
_____
_____
_____
_____
_____

Review Listen to each group of words. Then write the contraction for the words on the line.

1. _____

2. _____

3. _____

4. _____

Listen to each group of words. Then write the possessive noun and its object on the line.

5. _____

6. _____

7. _____

8. _____

Lesson 4

Writing Direct Quotations

Remember Conversation is written in a special way. **Quotation marks (" ")** are used before and after each direct quotation. A **comma (,)** is used to separate the **conversation words** from the direct quotation. When the conversation words come before the direct quotation, the end punctuation comes before the final quotation marks. When they come after the quotation, a declarative or imperative quotation ends with a comma.

Zhen said, "Name the primary colors."
"They are red, yellow, and blue," replied Cai.
"How many other colors are there?" asked Zhen.
Cai exclaimed, "What a good question that is!"

Think About In what kinds of quotations does the end punctuation remain the same whether the quotation comes before or after the speaker?

Read and Apply Read the conversation. Put commas, quotation marks, and end punctuation where they belong.

Aliya asked Have you ever seen a bat

How they scare me exclaimed Morgan

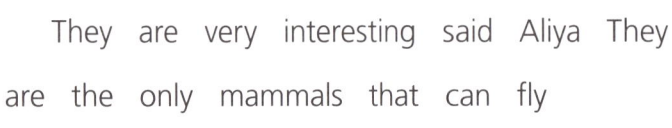

They are very interesting said Aliya They are the only mammals that can fly

Don't they get caught in people's hair Morgan asked

Aliya answered That is not true They have their own sonar system to help them fly during the night

Morgan said Maybe they aren't as scary as I thought

There are more than 1,000 species of bats in the world Aliya said Many of them eat insects How glad I am that they eat mosquitoes That is a good reason to like bats

Write About

Rewrite the conversation correctly. Remember to indent to start a new paragraph whenever the speaker changes. Add the correct punctuation.

Allan asked What is a food chain Blake explained It's a list of plants and animals where each animal eats the animal or plant below it on the list Everything has its place in the food chain added Malik Blake said The chain begins with green plants That's because they make their own food said Malik

Review

Rewrite each quotation correctly.

1. "What an amazing view"! exclaimed Tony.

2. "Neve asked," Why do we need to leave now?

3. "Do you know what time it is," wondered Ali?

4. Jasmine said. "This is my favorite book".

91

Lesson 5: Colon, Semicolon, and Dash

Remember   A **colon (:)** is used to introduce a list.

These are the things we need for breakfast: bread, jam, orange juice, cereal, and milk.

A **semicolon (;)** can be used to join two independent clauses in a compound sentence. It is used in place of a comma and a conjunction.

Hugh trained for months; he ran his first marathon yesterday.

A **dash (—)** sets off information that interrupts a sentence.

The roller coaster ride—his first ever—made his heart race.

Think About   Where are these three punctuation marks found in a sentence?

Read and Apply   Read the sentences. Insert colons, semicolons, and dashes where needed.

There are five Great Lakes Superior, Michigan, Huron, Ontario, and Erie. The lakes hold 20 percent of the freshwater on Earth they cover over 95,000 square miles. Of the lakes, Superior is the largest and the deepest. Erie is the shallowest it's only about 62 feet deep and the warmest. Important cities are near the Great Lakes Chicago, Toronto, Cleveland, Detroit, and Green Bay. Ships sail from these cities through the Great Lakes they travel to the Atlantic Ocean. People visit the Lakes for many things boating, swimming, fishing, and even surfing. Many people go to Niagara Falls it is between Lake Erie and Lake Ontario to see the famous waterfalls.

Great Lakes
Lake Superior, Lake Huron, Lake Ontario, Lake Michigan, Lake Erie

92

© The Continental Press, Inc.   **DUPLICATING THIS MATERIAL IS ILLEGAL.**

Write About   Write a paragraph about a visit to the beach. It can be real or imaginary. Use at least two of these punctuation marks: colon, semicolon, and dash.

_____
_____
_____
_____
_____
_____
_____
_____
_____

Review   Read each sentence. Write **C** if the sentence is correct as written. If there are errors, rewrite it correctly on the line.

1. We plan to visit the White House; then we will see the Capitol Building.
   _____

2. These are the things we need at the store; apples; bananas; spaghetti; and sauce.
   _____

3. Justin's—new bike it is red and blue—was in the garage.
   _____

4. Paige wants to be a doctor—Krista hopes to be an engineer.
   _____

5. Mr. Santana plays these instruments: piano, guitar, and trumpet.
   _____

Lesson 6: Writing Titles of Works

Remember Titles of works are written in a special way. Titles of books, newspapers, magazines, plays, and movies are underlined. Titles of stories, poems, songs, and TV and radio shows are put in **quotation marks (" ")**.

- Book <u>Sarah, Plain and Tall</u>
- Newspaper <u>The Dallas Morning News</u>
- Story "Raymond's Run"
- Song "Don't Worry, Be Happy"

Think About What is the difference between works whose titles are underlined and works whose titles are put in quotation marks?

_____

_____

Read and Apply Read the sentences. Punctuate each title correctly.

Sir Arthur Conan Doyle created the character Sherlock Holmes in the 1880s. This private detective first appeared in the novel A Study in Scarlet. Soon stories of his adventures were being published in The Strand Magazine. Holmes became famous for his ability to observe a situation and pick up clues that always helped him solve the case. Some of his most famous stories are The Red-Headed League and A Scandal in Bohemia.

Modern audiences still love Holmes. He has starred in many movies, including Sherlock Holmes. The TV shows Sherlock and Elementary are both modern spins on the detective's adventures. He's even been mentioned in songs like Dr. Watson and Mr. Holmes by Spirits of Rhythm and Sherlock Holmes by the band Sparks.

Write About Write a paragraph about the books and magazines your family enjoys reading and the movies and TV shows you like to watch.

_____
_____
_____
_____
_____
_____
_____
_____
_____

Review Read each sentence. Write **C** on the line if the title is punctuated correctly. Write **N** if it is not.

1. Matsuko saw "A Raisin in the Sun" at Hanson Theater. _____

2. Have you read the book Number the Stars? _____

3. My mom reads the "Washington Post" every day. _____

4. The poem Jabberwocky was written by Lewis Carroll. _____

5. We sing "Take Me Out to the Ball Game" in the seventh inning. _____

6. Dad and I saw "Finding Dory" in the theater. _____

7. Life was a magazine that used photographs to tell stories. _____

8. Did you watch "American Idol" last night? _____

Lesson 1

UNIT 9: Choosing the Right Word
Homophones

Remember   **Homophones** are words that sound alike, but are spelled differently and have different meanings.

Their means "belonging to them." *There* means "in that place." *They're* means "they are."

They're leaving in **their** car. They will be **there** in 10 minutes.

Two means "the number 2." *To* means "toward" or is used with verbs. *Too* means "more than enough" or "also."

The **two** of us want **to** go **to** the restaurant, **too**.

Your means "belonging to you." *You're* means "you are."

You're standing beside **your** desk.

Its is the possessive form of *it*. *It's* means "it is."

Where is the dog? **It's** time for **its** bath.

Think About   How can you remember the difference between *its* and *it's*?

Read and Apply   Read the sentences. Circle the correct homophone in each set.

[There   Their] are [to   two] solenodon species in the world. They live on the [two   too] islands of Cuba and Hispaniola. Solenodons use [their   they're] flexible snouts [too   to] find food. [There   They're] venomous mammals. A solenodon injects [it's   its] venom using special teeth. If [you're   your] visiting the solenodons' island home, [it's   its] not likely that you will see one. [Their   They're] nocturnal, so they sleep in [their   there] burrows during the day. When a solenodon comes out at night, [its   it's] tiny eyes do not help it much. It uses [it's   its] senses of hearing, touch, and smell [too   to] get around. Use [your   you're] computer to find a picture of these unusual animals.

© The Continental Press, Inc.   **DUPLICATING THIS MATERIAL IS ILLEGAL.**

Write About Write a sentence for each homophone.

1. it's
   _____

2. their
   _____

3. you're
   _____

4. too
   _____

5. they're
   _____

6. its
   _____

7. to
   _____

8. there
   _____

Review Circle the incorrect homophone in each sentence. Write the correct word on the line.

1. You're shoes are over there.   _____

2. It's two cold to go outside.   _____

3. The girls wanted to plan there party.   _____

4. My cat hates too wear its collar.   _____

5. Their waiting for your paper.   _____

© The Continental Press, Inc.   **DUPLICATING THIS MATERIAL IS ILLEGAL.**

Lesson 2: More Homophones

Remember Homophones are words that sound alike, but are spelled differently and have different meanings.

We stayed at an inn in Pennsylvania.

You see the sea from this hill.

Think About What are the different meanings of the homophones in the examples? How can you tell which word to use?

_____
_____
_____

Read and Apply Read the sentences. Circle the correct homophone.

In 1787, 55 men met to [right   write] a constitution [for   four] our [knew   new] country. They discussed [their   there] ideas. Some of the men thought a large state should have more power than a small [won   one]. Others would not [here   hear] of it. Since they could [not   knot] agree on [which   witch] way was best, they divided Congress into [to   two   too] parts. The number of representatives [in   inn] the House of Representatives depends on a state's population. But every state has a [pair   pear] of senators in the Senate. The groups must work together to make laws.

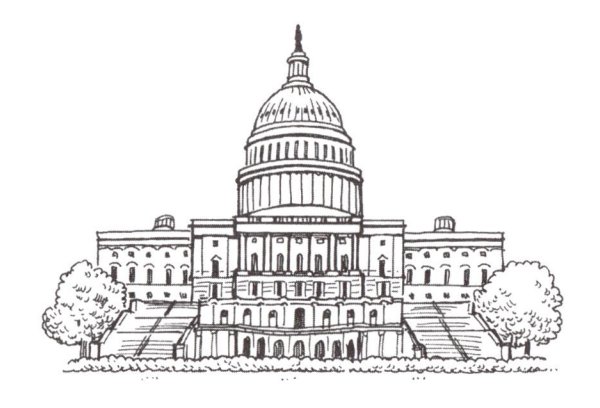

Write About Write two sentences for each pair of homophones.

1. rode/road

   _____
   _____

2. scent/sent

   _____
   _____

3. ate/eight

   _____
   _____

4. mane/main

   _____
   _____

5. ant/aunt

   _____
   _____

Review Use the homophones in the box to complete the sentences. You will not use all the words.

| pause | feet | poor | so |
| paws | feat | pour | sew |

1. Jared will _____ lemonade for everyone.

2. Please _____ for a moment of silence.

3. Mom can _____ my costume for the play.

4. My _____ will not fit in these shoes.

Lesson 3

Avoiding Double Negatives

Remember Some words mean "no." These include *no, not, nothing, nobody, none,* and *never.* Other negative words include *hardly, barely,* and *scarcely.* Only one of these words should be used in a sentence. This is true even when the word *not* is part of a contraction.

Incorrect   I can't see nothing here.

Correct   I can't see anything here.   OR   I can see nothing here.

Think About Read the examples again. What does *can't see nothing* actually mean?

_____

_____

Read and Apply Read the sentences. Correct the sentences that have double negatives by crossing out one of the words that means "no." Write a new word above it if necessary.

Nobody never sees a fangtooth in the ocean. These scary-looking fish don't never come close to the surface. They live around 16,000 feet underwater. Their name comes from their long, sharp teeth that show in their huge mouths. Don't not let those teeth scare you, though. A fangtooth isn't barely longer than six inches. These fish aren't never harmful to people. They don't eat nothing but small fish. They can't hardly see. Some scientists think a fangtooth finds its food by bumping into it. A fangtooth isn't nothing like other deep-sea fish. Scientists have been able to keep them alive in aquariums. People can't hardly understand how the fangtooth survives at extreme depths and can also adapt to live in aquariums.

© The Continental Press, Inc.   **DUPLICATING THIS MATERIAL IS ILLEGAL.**

Write About   Read these sentences. Rewrite the sentences correctly by removing the double negative.

1. There isn't nothing to prove that the man is the thief.
   _____

2. I can't hardly finish this sandwich.
   _____

3. Ripa couldn't find her coat nowhere.
   _____

4. I won't never go on that roller coaster again!
   _____

5. This milk doesn't taste no good.
   _____

6. Kaitlyn didn't tell no one her secret.
   _____

Review   Listen to each sentence. Circle **YES** if the sentence is correct. Circle **NO** if the sentence has a double negative in it.

1.   YES   NO
2.   YES   NO
3.   YES   NO
4.   YES   NO
5.   YES   NO

© The Continental Press, Inc.   **DUPLICATING THIS MATERIAL IS ILLEGAL.**

Lesson 4: Misused Words

Remember The word *good* is always an adjective. The word *well* is usually an adverb. It is an adjective only when it means "healthy."

Nadine was a <u>good</u> runner before she hurt her knee.
She could run <u>well</u> even on sand.
She'll be running again as soon as she is <u>well</u>.

The word *can* means "to be able to." The word *may* means "to be allowed to." *May* is also used to show that something is possible or likely.

I <u>can</u> jump high.
You <u>may</u> not jump off that fence because you <u>may</u> hurt yourself.

The word *have* can be a helping verb that is used with other verbs. Never use the preposition *of* when you mean *have*.

             have
We should ~~of~~ taken the train.

Think About Look at the first set of examples again. What does *well* tell about in the second sentence and in the third sentence?

_____

Read and Apply Read the sentences. Find the five misused words. Cross out each word and write the correct word above it.

In order to think good, you need energy. Energy comes from eating good food and getting exercise. You should of heard of the three parts of fitness: endurance, strength, and flexibility. Endurance comes from aerobic exercise. You can ride bike, play soccer, roller skate, swim, or run. To have good strength, you must work your muscles good. Exercises like push-ups, crunches, and pull-ups are well for making strong muscles. You may use stretches to become more flexible. Then your muscles and joints can bend and move well.

Write About Use each word correctly in a sentence.

1. good
   _____

2. may
   _____

3. well
   _____

4. can
   _____

5. have
   _____

Review Read each sentence. Write **C** on the line if the sentence is correct. Write **N** on the line if a word is misused in the sentence.

1. Nick had a cold but is good now.   _____

2. You could of called to say you'd be late.   _____

3. We can have ice cream after dinner.   _____

4. Can I go home early?   _____

5. Hollie may go outside after she does her homework.   _____

6. Trevor plays soccer well.   _____

7. You can eat some of the grapes.   _____

8. I should have closed the window when it rained.   _____

© The Continental Press, Inc.   **DUPLICATING THIS MATERIAL IS ILLEGAL.**

Lesson 5: More Misused Words

Remember The adjective *those* points out a noun. The object pronoun *them* should never be used as an adjective.

Incorrect A carpenter built <u>them</u> bookshelves.

Correct A carpenter built <u>those</u> bookshelves.

Who is a pronoun used as a subject of a sentence or a clause. The subject is the doer or actor. *Whom* is a pronoun used as an object in a sentence or a clause. It will usually be a direct object or an object of a preposition.

<u>Who</u> fixed the broken lock?
I think I know <u>who</u> did it.

<u>Whom</u> do you believe?
Yumiko is the one to <u>whom</u> this letter is addressed.

Think About Read the first set of examples again. Why can't *them* be used to tell about *bookshelves*?

_____

Read and Apply Read the sentences. Find five misused words. Cross out each word and write the correct word above it.

Do you know whom Hercules was? Hercules was a half god and half man who appears in ancient Greek stories. When Hercules was a baby, the goddess Hera put snakes in his crib. He strangled them snakes with his bare hands! Hera tricked him into doing horrible things. Afterward, Hercules felt awful. He visited an oracle, a person to who the future was known. An oracle did not give clear answers to them people whom asked. This oracle told Hercules that he needed to complete 12 very difficult tasks. When he did those tasks, he would be forgiven.

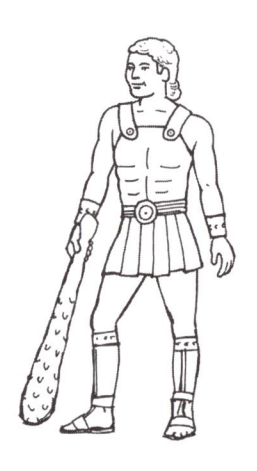

Write About Write a sentence using each word correctly.

1. those

   _____
   _____

2. them

   _____
   _____

3. who

   _____
   _____

4. whom

   _____
   _____

Review Read each sentence. Write **C** on the line if the sentence is correct. Write **N** on the line if a word is misused in the sentence.

1. Them egrets are very graceful. _____

2. Who needs a napkin? _____

3. Clara is the person to whom you should give the paper. _____

4. My sister made those cookies. _____

5. This is the author whom wrote my favorite book. _____

6. I found them socks in the living room. _____

UNIT 10: Writing Letters
Writing a Thank-You Note

Remember A **thank-you note** is a type of friendly letter that thanks someone for a gift or for doing something. It has five parts. The **heading** is the writer's address and the date on which the letter was written. The **greeting** says hello to the person who gets the letter. The **body** is the message of the letter. The **closing** says good-bye. The **signature** is the handwritten name of the writer. Use **commas** and capital letters correctly in a thank-you note.

heading { 215 Oak Grove Road
Durham, NC 27702
October 10, 2016

Dear April, } greeting

Thank you for inviting me to your house last weekend. I had a great time and I enjoyed playing a new game. Thank you for having me. I hope you can visit me soon. } body

Your friend, } closing
Tiffany } signature

Think About Who is a thank-you note written to and what does it say?

_____

_____

Read and Apply Read this thank-you note. Label each part of the letter. Underline what the writer thought was special.

_____ → 16 Fifth Street
Baltimore, MD 21224
July 6, 2016

Dear Bret, ← _____

Thank you for taking me to the Orioles' game on Saturday. I had a great time. It was so exciting to see the Orioles win in the ninth inning. ← _____

_____ → Your friend,
_____ → David

106

Write About Write a thank-you note to someone who has done something special for you. Write your address and today's date in the heading.

_____
_____
_____
_____
_____
_____
_____
_____
_____
_____
_____
_____
_____
_____
_____
_____
_____
_____
_____

Review Read the body of each thank-you note. Cross out the information that is not needed.

1. Thank you for the new video game and for coming to my birthday party. I hope you had fun. I really wanted to have a pool party instead. I can't wait to play this new game. It looks like a blast!

2. Thank you for taking me to the art museum on Sunday. I learned a lot about different artists. I really enjoyed looking at the gallery of Italian painters. I wish there were more paintings about sports. I hope we can go again sometime!

Lesson 2: Writing a Business Letter

Remember A **business letter** has one more part than a friendly letter. The **inside address** gives the name and address of the person or company receiving the letter. In the signature, the writer usually signs and prints his or her name.

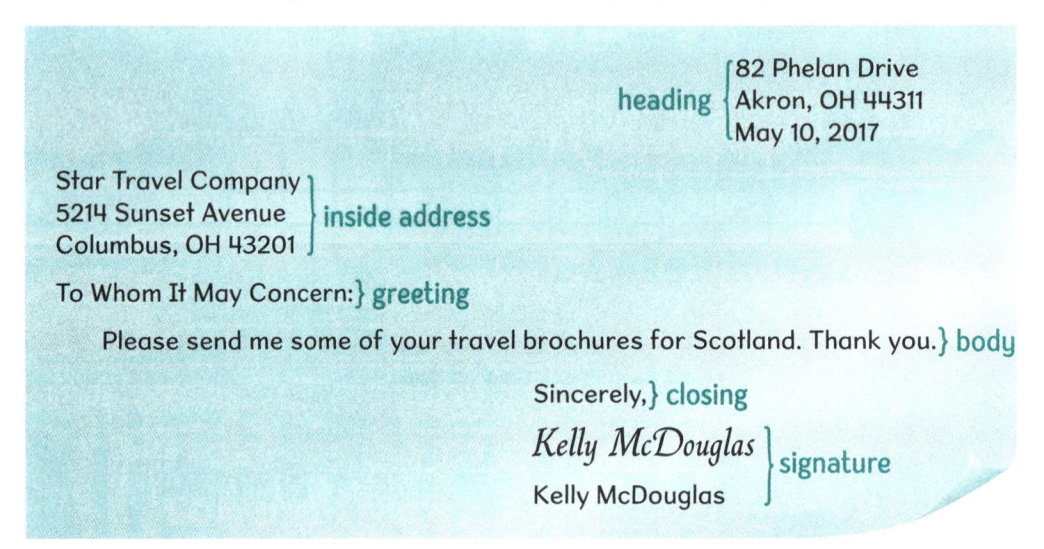

> **heading:**
> 82 Phelan Drive
> Akron, OH 44311
> May 10, 2017
>
> **inside address:**
> Star Travel Company
> 5214 Sunset Avenue
> Columbus, OH 43201
>
> **greeting:** To Whom It May Concern:
>
> **body:** Please send me some of your travel brochures for Scotland. Thank you.
>
> **closing:** Sincerely,
>
> **signature:**
> *Kelly McDouglas*
> Kelly McDouglas

Think About What punctuation mark is used after the greeting in a business letter?

_____

Read and Apply Read this business letter. Label each part of the letter.

> _____ → 53 Derby Lane
> Austin, TX 78703
> March 23, 2017
>
> Mr. Henry Jones
> Run for Fun
> 637 Front Street ← _____
> Austin, TX 78703
>
> Dear Mr. Jones: ← _____
>
> I am the president of my school's Community Service Club. We want to help during the Run for Fun next month. Please contact me with details. Thank you. ← _____
>
> _____ → Sincerely,
> _____ → *Emilio Gomez*
> Emilio Gomez

Write About Write a business letter. Use your address and today's date in the heading. Write a letter to the subscription department of *Animal Fun Magazine* at P.O. Box 25635 in Dallas, TX. The zip code is 75002. In the body of the letter, tell the person that you want to stop getting the magazine. Give a reason why. Include all the parts of a business letter.

_____
_____
_____
_____
_____
_____
_____
_____
_____
_____
_____
_____
_____

Review Look at the business letter in Read and Apply. Answer these questions about that letter.

1. Who wrote the letter? _____

2. When was the letter sent? _____

3. What company is receiving the letter? _____

4. What person is receiving the letter? _____

5. How is the signature different from the signature of a friendly letter? _____
_____

© The Continental Press, Inc. **DUPLICATING THIS MATERIAL IS ILLEGAL.**

109

Lesson 3: Addressing an Envelope

Remember Mail a letter in an envelope. The **return address** goes in the upper left corner. This is the name and address of the person who wrote the letter. The **mailing address** goes in the middle. This is the name and address of the person who will receive the letter. A stamp goes in the upper right corner. Use commas to separate the city and state in an address. Use capital letters for proper nouns.

Return Address:
Jennifer Larson
85 Crescent St.
Mobile, AL 33605

Mailing Address:
Mr. Gene Johns, President
Pear Computer Company
116 Third Ave.
New York, NY 10001

Stamp →

Think About What is the return address, and why is it important to put it on the envelope?

_____

_____

Read and Apply Read the envelope below. Circle the letters that should be capitals. Add commas where they belong.

Tim Delgado
153 north 4th street
Boulder CO 80911

Mrs. Laura greenberg
21 Caballero ave
wabash, in 46992

110

Write About Address the envelope below. Use your own name and address for the return address. For the mailing address write this name and address correctly: ms. diana foster, friends of animals club, 1 pine st. neptune, nj 07753. Draw a stamp in the correct place.

Review Look at the envelope below. Write the correct letter to show what goes in each spot. Not all the letters will be used.

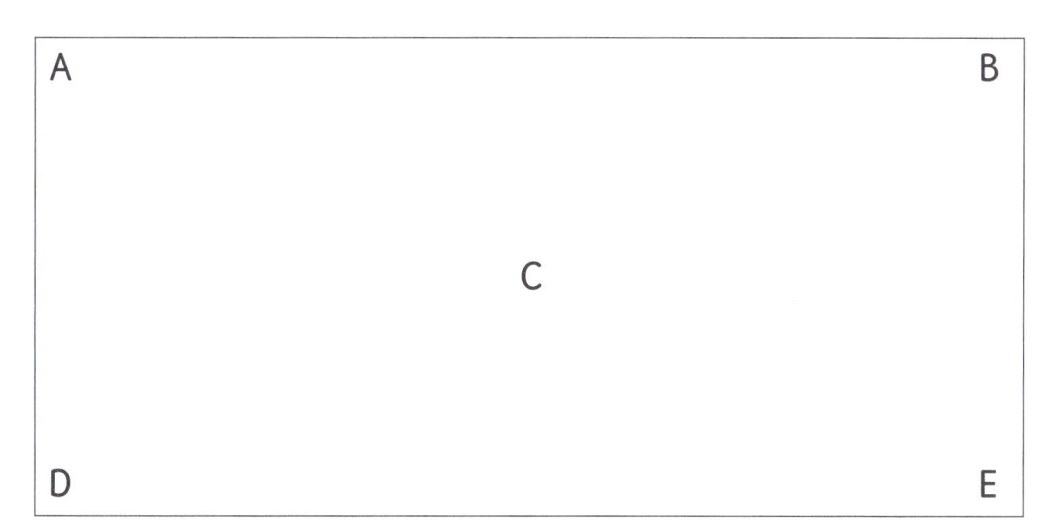

1. Stamp _____

2. Return Address _____

3. Mailing Address _____

Lesson 4: Writing an Email

Remember It is often easier and faster to communicate through email. When writing an email, it is still important to use proper grammar. The **subject line** of the email should clearly state what the email is about.

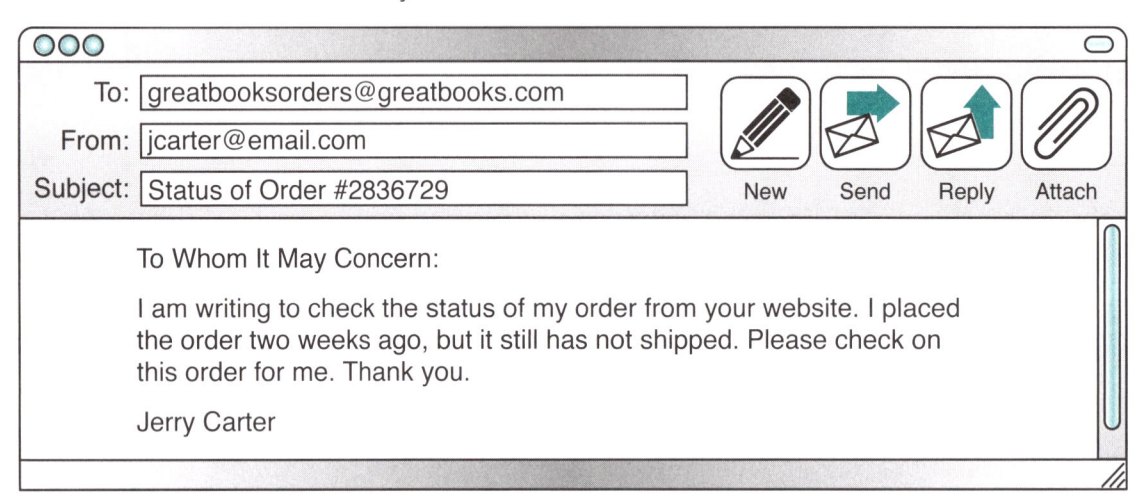

```
To: greatbooksorders@greatbooks.com
From: jcarter@email.com
Subject: Status of Order #2836729

To Whom It May Concern:

I am writing to check the status of my order from your website. I placed the order two weeks ago, but it still has not shipped. Please check on this order for me. Thank you.

Jerry Carter
```

Think About What parts of a friendly or business letter are not needed in an email?

_____

Read and Apply Read the email. Answer the questions below.

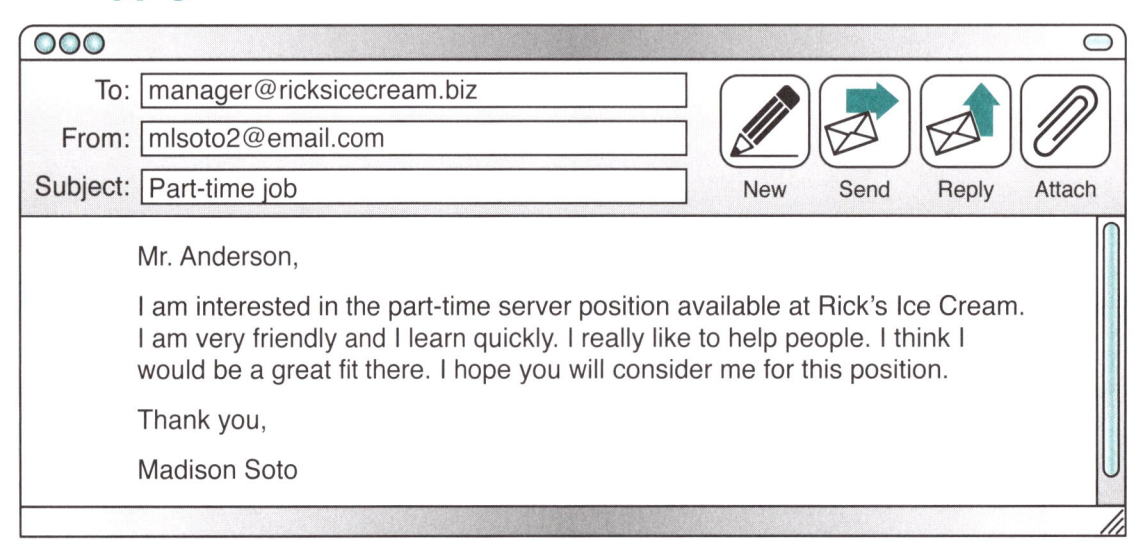

```
To: manager@ricksicecream.biz
From: mlsoto2@email.com
Subject: Part-time job

Mr. Anderson,

I am interested in the part-time server position available at Rick's Ice Cream. I am very friendly and I learn quickly. I really like to help people. I think I would be a great fit there. I hope you will consider me for this position.

Thank you,

Madison Soto
```

1. Who is sending the email? _____

2. Why is the email being sent? _____

3. What is the subject line? _____

Write About Write an email to the manager of Corner Bakery thanking them for their donation to your basketball team's bake sale. Include an appropriate subject line. Create an email address using your name.

To: manager@cornerbakery.biz
From:
Subject:

New   Send   Reply   Attach

Review Read this text from an email. Put end punctuations marks and commas where they belong. Circle letters that should be capitals.

Miss bucher

thank you for my piano lesson yesterday i learned a lot and i am really excited to work on this new song when is my recital i want to invite my grandparents my aunt my uncle and my parents

thank you

Jerome Black

Grammar Handbook

Abbreviation — a short way to write a word, usually ending in a period. Abbreviations for proper nouns begin with a capital letter.

> *Examples:* Jan.   Thurs.   Rd.

Abstract Noun — a noun that you cannot see, smell, taste, touch, or hear

> *Examples:* friendship   loyalty   pride

Action Verb — a word that tells about doing something

> *Examples:* grin   imagines   went

Adjective — a word that describes a noun by telling how many, what color, what size or what kind

> *Examples:* three bikes   tiny cat

Adverb — a word that describes a verb by telling how, when, or where something happened; it also modifies adjectives and other adverbs

> *Examples:* run slowly   play today   very rich

Apostrophe — a punctuation mark that takes the place of letters left out of a contraction or makes a possessive form

Articles — the special adjectives *a, an,* and *the*

Body — the main part of a letter

Business Letter — a letter written to someone the sender does not know for a reason that is not personal

Clause — a group of words that has a subject and a predicate

Closing — the part of a letter that says good-bye

Colon — a punctuation mark used to introduce a list; also used after the greeting in a business letter

Comma — a punctuation mark that separates things or ideas

Common Noun	a word that names any person, place, animal, or thing
	Examples: boy park cat
Comparative	form of an adjective or adverb that compares two
Complete Predicate	the simple predicate and all the words that tell about it
Complete Subject	the simple subject and all the words that tell about it
Complex Sentence	a sentence with an independent clause and at least one dependent clause
Compound Predicate	two predicates joined together in one sentence with the word *and*
Compound Sentence	two sentences joined together with the word *and, but,* or *or*
Compound Subject	two subjects joined together in one sentence with the word *and*
Conjunction	a connecting word
	Examples: and or but
Contraction	two words combined into one by using an apostrophe to take the place of the letters left out
	Examples: he'll wouldn't can't
Conversation Words	words used to indicate that a person is speaking
	Examples: said asked wondered
Correlative Conjunctions	conjunctions that are used in pairs to connect two grammatically equivalent parts of a sentence
	Example: neither milk nor sugar
Dash	a punctuation mark used to show a break in the flow of a sentence
Declarative Sentence	a sentence that tells something
Dependent Clause	part of a sentence that has a subject and a predicate but does not make sense by itself
Direct Object	a noun or pronoun that receives the action of an action verb
Direct Quotation	the exact words that someone said

Exclamation Point	the punctuation mark used at the end of an exclamatory sentence
Exclamatory Sentence	a sentence that shows strong feeling
Fragment	a group of words that does not tell a complete thought
Future Tense	verb tense that tells about action that will happen later
Greeting	the part near the beginning of a letter that names the person receiving it
Heading	the part at the beginning of a letter that gives the writer's address and the date the letter was written
Helping Verb	a verb that helps a main verb tell about an action

> *Examples:* has arrived   is sleeping

Homophones	words that sound alike, but are spelled differently and have different meanings
Imperative Sentence	a sentence that tells or commands someone to do something
Independent Clause	part of a sentence with a subject and a predicate that makes sense by itself
Initial	the first letter of a name
Inside Address	the name and address of the person receiving a business letter
Interjection	a word that shows strong or sudden feeling
Interrogative Sentence	a sentence that asks a question
Linking Verb	a verb that tells about being something, does not show action

> *Examples:* is   were   are

Mailing Address	the address a letter is being sent to
Main Verb	the most important verb in a sentence
Misplaced Modifier	a modifier that is poorly placed in a sentence and causes confusion
Modifier	a word or group of words that adds details to a sentence

Object of a Preposition	the noun or pronoun that follows a preposition
Object Pronoun	form of a pronoun that the action is happening to
Past Participle	a special past-tense verb form used with the helping verbs *has, have,* and *had*
Past Tense	verb tense that tells about action that already happened
Perfect Tense	verb tense that uses helping verbs and the past participle of the main verb to describe action
Period	the punctuation mark used at the end of a declarative or imperative sentence and most abbreviations
Plural Noun	a noun that names more than one person, place, animal, or thing

Examples: trees   benches   children

Possessive Noun	a noun that names who or what something belongs to

Examples: Jody's desk   dogs' bones

Possessive Pronoun	a pronoun that names who or what something belongs to

Examples: my shoes   its tail

Predicate	the part of a sentence that tells what the subject does or is
Preposition	a word that relates the noun or pronoun that follows it to another word in the sentence

Examples: after   by   from   with

Prepositional Phrase	a preposition, the noun or pronoun that follows it, and all the words that come between them
Present Participle	a special verb form made by adding *ing* to the verb that is used with a helping verb
Present Tense	verb tense that describes action taking place now
Progressive Tense	verb tense that uses a helping verb and the present participle of the main verb to show continuing action
Pronoun	a word that can take the place of a noun

Examples: she   he   it

Proper Noun	a word that names a special person, place, animal, or thing

> *Examples:* Ellie   Nevada   Fido   *Mayflower*

Question Mark	the punctuation mark used at the end of an interrogative sentence
Quotation Marks	punctuation marks used before and after someone's exact words in a written conversation, and around the title of a short work
Referent	the noun that a pronoun takes the place of
Relative Pronoun	a pronoun that introduces a clause that describes

> *Examples:* which   that   who

Return Address	the address from which a letter is being sent
Run-On Sentence	a group of words that tells more than one complete thought
***Self*-Pronoun**	a pronoun that ends with *self* and refers back to the subject of the sentence

> *Examples:* yourself   myself   themselves

Semicolon	a punctuation mark used to join two independent clauses in a compound sentence
Sentence	a group of words that tells a complete thought and makes sense
Signature	the writer's name at the end of a letter
Simple Predicate	the verb or verb phrase that tells what the subject does or is
Simple Subject	the noun or pronoun that the sentence tells about
Singular Noun	a noun that names one person, place, animal, or thing

> *Examples:* tree   bench   child

Subject	the part of a sentence that tells who or what the sentence is about
Subject Line	the part of an email that tells what it is about
Subject Pronoun	form of a pronoun that appears in the subject part of a sentence
Superlative	form of an adjective or adverb that compares three or more

Thank-you Note a type of friendly letter expressing thanks

Title part of a person's name or the name of a book or story

> *Examples:*   Miss Brown   Dr. Sanchez
> *Alice in Wonderland*   "Cinderella"

Uncountable Nouns nouns that cannot be counted with numbers, always expressed as singular

> *Examples:*   soup   news   water

Verb Phrase the main verb and any helping verbs

> *Examples:*   were laughing   are running

USING CAPITAL LETTERS

- Begin every sentence with a capital letter.
- Begin each part of a person's name with a capital letter. Include titles that are used as part of the name and initials.
- Begin words that name days, months, holidays, and places with a capital letter. Do not capitalize the names of seasons.
- Begin abbreviations of proper nouns with a capital letter.

USING PUNCTUATION MARKS

End Marks

- End every sentence with a period (.), a question mark (?), or an exclamation point (!).
- End a statement with a period.
- End a question with a question mark.
- End an exclamation with an exclamation point.

Comma

- Use a comma before the joining word in a compound sentence.
- Use commas between words or phrases in a series.
- Use a comma between the day and year in a date.
- Use a comma between a city and state.

Apostrophe

- Use an apostrophe to show who owns or has something. If the owner is singular, add an apostrophe and *s*. If the owner is plural and ends in *s,* add just an apostrophe.
- Use an apostrophe to show where letters are missing in a contraction.

Quotation Marks

- Use quotation marks before and after a person's exact words.

Colon

- Use a colon to introduce a list in a sentence.
- Use a colon after the greeting of a business letter.

Semicolon
- Use a semicolon to separate two independent clauses in a compound sentence. The semicolon takes the place of a conjunction.

Dash
- Use a dash to show an interruption in the flow of a sentence. Dashes are used in pairs. Put one dash at the beginning of the interruption and one dash at the end.

Showing Titles
- Capitalize the first word, last word, and every important word in a title.
- Underline book titles
- Use quotation marks for shorter works, such as poems and articles.

USING CORRECT GRAMMAR

Subject-Verb Agreement
- When you use an action verb in the present tense, add *s* or *es* to the verb if the subject is a singular noun. Do not add *s* or *es* to the verb if the subject is plural.
- If the subject is a pronoun, add *s* or *es* to the verb only if the pronoun is *he, she,* or *it.*

Subject-Verb Agreement with Forms of *Be*
- If the subject is a singular noun, use *is* for the present tense and *was* for the past tense.
- If the subject is a plural noun or compound subject, use *are* for the present tense and *were* for the past tense.
- Use the correct form of *be* with a singular or plural pronoun subject.

Present Tense		Past Tense	
Singular	**Plural**	**Singular**	**Plural**
I am you are he, she, *or* it is	we are you are they are	I was you were he, she, *or* it was	we were you were they were

Irregular Verbs

- The verbs below and many others are called irregular because their past-tense forms do not end in *ed*. Use the correct past-tense forms of irregular verbs.

Present	Past	Past Participle
is	was	(has) been
begin	began	(has) begun
bring	brought	(has) brought
choose	chose	(has) chosen
come	came	(has) come
fly	flew	(has) flown
go	went	(has) gone
have	had	(has) had
know	knew	(has) known
make	made	(has) made
run	ran	(has) run
say	said	(has) said
speak	spoke	(has) spoken
take	took	(has) taken
wear	wore	(has) worn
write	wrote	(has) written

Subject and Object Pronouns

- Pronouns have different subject and object forms.
- Use subject pronouns as the subject of a sentence.
- Use object pronouns after an action verb or after a preposition such as *of, to, for,* or *about*. The pronouns *you* and *it* have only one form.

Subject		Object	
Singular	Plural	Singular	Plural
I he she	we they	me him her	us them

Naming Yourself Last

- When you speak of yourself and another person, name yourself last.

Possessive Pronouns

- Use these possessive pronouns before a noun to show ownership.

Singular	Plural
my your his, her, its	our your their

- Use these possessive pronouns when a noun does not follow.

Singular	Plural
mine yours his, hers, its	ours yours theirs

Tricky Words

- Some words are often confused. Remember to use these words correctly.

a/an	Use *a* before a consonant sound. Use *an* before a vowel sound. Wrong: **a** orange Correct: **an** orange

can/may	Use *can* to ask if or tell that you are able to do something. Use *may* to ask if or tell that something is possible or allowed.
	      Wrong: **Can** I borrow your pen?
	      Correct: **May** I borrow your pen?

good/well	Use *good* only as an adjective. Use *well* as an adverb unless you are describing someone's state of health.
	      Wrong: He pitches **good.**
	      Correct: He pitches **well.** He is a **good** pitcher.
	      Wrong: I have a cold and don't feel **good.**
	      Correct: I have a cold and don't feel **well.**

have/of	Use *have* or *'ve* after words such as *could, should,* and *would.* Do not use *of.*
	      Wrong: I could **of** gone.
	      Correct: I could **have** gone. I could**'ve** gone.

hear/here	*Hear* means "to be aware of sound": I **hear** music. *Here* means "in this place": Put your bags **here.**
its/it's	*Its* means "belonging to it": The dog wagged **its** tail. *It's* means "it is": **It's** raining.
lay/lie	*Lay* means "to put something in a certain place": She **lay** the note on the table. *Lie* means "to stretch out and rest": I **lie** down on my bed.

than/then	*Than* is a word for comparing: Today is hotter **than** yesterday. *Then* means "at that time" or "next": Raise one arm and **then** the other.
their/there/they're	*Their* means "belonging to them": They ate **their** dinner. *There* means "in that place": **There** you are! Sit over **there**. *They're* means "they are": **They're** the fastest runners.
those/them	*Those* is an adjective that points out a noun: Bring **those** books with you. *Them* is an object pronoun: I went to the game with **them.**

to/too/two	*To* means "toward" or "for the purpose of":
	   Go **to** the park **to** play.
	To can also be part of a verb form: She likes **to** skate.
	Too means "more than enough" or "also":
	   I ate **too** much. You did, **too.**
	Two means "the sum of 1 + 1": The cat had **two** kittens.

who/whom	*Who* is a pronoun used as a subject of a sentence or a clause:
	   Who found the key?
	   I know **who** found the key.
	Whom is a pronoun used as an object in a sentence or a clause:
	   Whom did you ask?
	   Morgan is the one **whom** I asked.

who's/whose	*Who's* means "who is": **Who's** coming to the party? *Whose* is the possessive form of who: I don't know **whose** hat this is.
your/you're	*Your* means "belonging to you": Put on **your** jacket. *You're* means "you are": **You're** late for the bus.

NOTES

NOTES